Welcoming Strangers

Welcoming Strangers

Nonviolent Re-parenting of Children in Foster Care

Jane Hall Fitz-Gibbon
Andrew Fitz-Gibbon

Transaction Publishers
New Brunswick (U.S.A.) and London (U.K.)

Library of Congress Catalog Number: 2015033901
ISBN: 978-1-4128-6276-9 (hardcover); 978-1-4128-6320-9 (paperback)
eBook: 978-1-4128-6226-4
Printed in the United States of America

Library of Congress Cataloging-in-Publication Data

Fitz-Gibbon, Jane (Jane Hall), author.
  Welcoming strangers : the loving nonviolent (re)parenting of children in foster care / Jane Hall Fitz-Gibbon and Andrew Fitz-Gibbon.
    pages cm
  Includes bibliographical references.
  ISBN 978-1-4128-6276-9 (hardcover : alk. paper)--ISBN 978-1-4128-6226-4 (e-book) 1. Foster children--United States. 2. Foster home care--United States. 3. Abused children--Services for--United States. 4. Child welfare--United States. I. Fitz-Gibbon, Andrew L., 1951- author. II. Title.
  HV881.F545 2015
  362.76'850973--dc23
                                                        2015033901

For Joey, who likely will not read this book, still . . .

Contents

Acknowledgments ix

A Note about Language xi

Introduction: Welcoming Strangers xiii

1 Responding to a Major Need 1

2 The Multiple Violences Suffered by Children in Care 11

3 Larger Houses, More Children 27

4 Thinking Further about Violence 37

5 Why Re-parenting? 47

6 Teens, Tantrums, Sex, and Substance Abuse 63

7 A Question of Ethics: How Shall We Live? 81

8 The Long Term: Permanence, Adoption, Returning
Home, and Keeping in Touch 95

9 Spanking, Discipline, and Nonviolence 107

10 Loving Nonviolent Habits and Virtues 121

11 Second-Hand Shock Syndrome and Caring for Yourself 139

12 Praxis: Creating a Nonviolent Home with the
Ordinariness of Love 155

Addendum: Money Can't Buy Me Love   161

Appendix: Definitions of Child Abuse, Maltreatment,
and Neglect in New York   167

References   173

Index   177

Acknowledgments

Over the thirty-three years of our life as foster carers so many people have helped and have been a part of the journey. To mention them all is not possible, and so with reluctance we resort to categories—thanks to the many caseworkers, case managers, foster carers, birth parents, adoptive parents, support staff from myriad agencies, and the children who have stayed with us for short and long periods. We are especially grateful to those who read the manuscript and gave helpful critique and comment: from the academy, Professors Karla Alwes, Mechthild Nagel, Kathryn Russell, and Patricia Martinez at the State University of New York College at Cortland, Danielle Poe at the University of Dayton, Barry Gan at St. Bonaventure's University, R. Paul Churchill at George Washington University, and Joseph Betz at Villanova University; and from social services and the general reading public, Shella Chase, Sierra Williams, Rebekah Donlan-Fitzgibbon, Jennifer Donlan-Fitzgibbon, Esq., Pamela Talbott. Thanks to Jake Gerard for graphics. Daniel Wasson at the Center for Development of Human Services (CDHS), Research Foundation of SUNY, Buffalo State College, deserves extra thanks for encouraging us along the way and supporting our being Visiting Scholars at CDHS during the writing of this book. Thanks, finally, to the anonymous reviewer and editors at Transaction Publications for helpful suggestions that made the text stronger.

A Note about Language

It is no longer acceptable in written English to use gender-restricted language when speaking generically—in other words, the use of "man," "men," "he," or "his" is not satisfactory when speaking about male and female or females only. Because of the long history of the usage of sexist generic language, writers are presented with a challenge. With regard to personal pronouns, one solution is to use the plural—they and their. This makes grammar problematical. Another solution, which we have adopted, is to alternate "she" and "he" when speaking generically. However, a few times in the text we deliberately use "she" to disrupt convention and stereotypes.

Throughout the book we use "foster carer" rather than "foster parent." We do this for three reasons. First, we first began our fostering career in the United Kingdom where the common term is "carer" rather than "parent." In part, this is to recognize consciously that children in the care of others have birth parents with whom the children often have deep attachment. Second, in part, this book looks at ethics and underlying much that we say is the "ethics of care," a way of thinking about ethics that sees the caring relationships as foundational for morality. Third, we coin the term "re-parenting" to describe the task of the foster carer, and make a distinction between the role of parent and carer and the function of parenting or re-parenting. For example, a grandparent may become the carer of a child who re-parents the grandchild.

We have avoided the use of jargon—philosophical, psychological, professional—as far as possible. One exception is the term "hotline," a shorthand term to refer to the process of mandatory reporting of suspected child neglect or abuse by certain mandated reporters or members of the public. "Hotline" has become a common term used by people and agencies involved in the care of children (e.g., some schools have "hotline training" and agencies have "hotline regulations"). In time the term has morphed from a noun to an inelegant, but descriptive, verb "to hotline," as in "we hotlined the birth parents." In this regard, we beg the reader's indulgence!

Introduction:
Welcoming Strangers

stranger |'strānjər|

noun

a person whom one does not know or
with whom one is not familiar: *don't talk to strangers*
—Apple Dictionary

The ancient Greek philosopher Plato believed that when children are
born they come to us from another place. The newborn looks around,
not comprehending this strange world. The realm of the perfect is
left behind and the new human is pushed, and sometimes pulled,
into the world. Memories of the perfect are still vivid, but the infant
cannot communicate with the new world. By the time she can, her
memories of the other world are fading. She continues to act out the
other world in her imagination and in her playing. Soon she begins to
forget. Becoming an adult is to forget finally and almost completely
the other world. The saints and sages and adepts of all ages and places
learn the secrets of reconnecting. Yet even they have only rare glimpses
and shadowy memories. Most of us seeing and remembering, as if
catching something out of the corner of an eye, quickly dismiss it as
mere whimsy.

Plato's myth helps our imagination. If the world is strange to the
newborn, it is clear that the newborn is also a stranger to the world.
She is a stranger even to her parents—perhaps less so to her mother
who has nurtured and carried her for nine months. Yet, even for mom
the baby is a stranger still to be known. For parents, learning to know
the infant begins immediately. Gradually she ceases to be a stranger.
As she grows, she will still surprise, but the surprises are more often

than not tinged with familiarity. Andy remembers, on seeing our firstborn, thinking, "So that's what you look like! Of course you do!" Despite the strangeness, there was something familiar—mystically so perhaps. Genetic connections are difficult to classify, but nonetheless real.

Even so, all children come to us as strangers. The strangeness is compounded when we care for the children of others. In caring for children from birth, besides the genetic connection, we more or less know the socialization process they pass through—at least so in the early years before the state takes a primary role through the public school system. Not knowing and feeling the genetic connection, and unsure what socialization processes a child has passed through, makes the child more of a stranger to us. When the ever so crucial early years are accompanied by neglect, abuse, trauma, and violence, then strangeness is magnified. Trauma and violence have unpredictable effect.

There are two narratives concerning strangers. The first is that the stranger is a threat to us, not to be trusted. "Don't talk to strangers," "Never accept a ride from a stranger," we tell our children. When someone we do not know stops us in the street, often our first reaction is one of guardedness as we check out the genuineness of the new person. Our sympathetic nervous system takes over: heartbeat gets faster, muscles tense, tummy flutters, breath becomes shorter as the primitive fight or flight response kicks in. A guarded defensiveness might turn to a smile when we realize that this stranger is not a threat, for he is not a person of whom to be afraid.

The second narrative of the stranger is to provide hospitality to others, for we are all strangers. The Golden Rule, "Do to others as you would have them do to you," dictates that we provide hospitality and care for the stranger, for we too would want that for ourselves. The New Testament suggests that in welcoming strangers we may well-entertain angels. Strangers need our care.

For more than thirty years, we have tried to live in the second narrative. We have welcomed children as strangers into our home to provide hospitality and care. We have done so as part of the social system of foster care that includes careful training and retraining, certification and oversight, with associated rules and requirements. Local authorities administer foster care, more often than not, though there are private agencies. State sponsored or private, foster care has strict legal requirements and guidelines that govern agencies, birth families, children in care, and foster carers alike. For those on the "inside," this is known colloquially as "the system." We have been certified foster carers both in the United Kingdom and the United States, working with four different departments of social services in different towns and cities. We have cared for over a hundred children. These children have ranged in age from six-hour-old to a couple of twenty-year-olds. They have come to us because of basic parental neglect, and because of the most egregious physical, emotional, and sexual abuse imaginable.

In New York State, according to the Office of Children and Family Services (NYSOCFS n.d.):

> Generally, the term abuse encompasses the most serious harms committed against children. An "abused child" is a child whose parent or other person legally responsible for his/her care inflicts upon the child serious physical injury, creates a substantial risk of serious physical injury, or commits an act of sex abuse against the child. Not only can a person be abusive to a child if they perpetrate any of these actions against a child in their care, they can be guilty of abusing a child if they allow someone else to do these things to that child.
>
> Maltreatment refers to the quality of care a child is receiving from those responsible for him/her. Maltreatment occurs when a parent or other person legally responsible for the care of a child harms a child, or places a child in imminent danger of harm by failing to exercise the minimum degree of care in providing the child with any of the following: food, clothing, shelter, education, or medical care when financially able to do so. Maltreatment can also result from abandonment of a child or from not providing adequate supervision for the child. Further, a child may be maltreated if a parent engages in excessive use of drugs or alcohol such that it interferes with their ability to adequately supervise the child. (See Appendix for the legal definitions of abuse, maltreatment, and neglect.)

We have cared for children across the whole spectrum of neglect, maltreatment, and abuse. Children have stayed in our home for anything from a few days to six years. The most children we have cared for has been six at any one time, besides our own three birth children. Over the years, we have been involved in training courses for new foster carers and adopters, and have taught courses on child sexual abuse (Jane more so than Andy). We have known many hundreds of other foster carers and caseworkers, and have learned much from them.

We came to foster care with the primary motivation of wanting to give something back to society, a form of civic responsibility. We both enjoyed the benefits of loving parents who did a reasonable job of seeing us through to adulthood. Neither of us suffered deprivation of any kind. Nor did we experience physical, emotional, or sexual abuse. Our memories of childhood are good ones. We make no pretense that our parents were perfect. Just that like most parents, they faced the task of parenthood with courage, good grace, and humor. They did their best, and we turned out okay.

We became aware that not all young children have the kinds of childhood experiences that we had both enjoyed. We had two little boys of our own—our daughter would join us a few years later—and like our parents before us, we muddled through, learning as we went along. Our little ones were doing well. Why wouldn't we try to share what we were learning with those with a variety of needs?

There are many ways of "giving back." Some volunteer in soup kitchens, some agitate for change through social activism, some apply their skills in the administration of not-for-profit organizations, and some serve in the local fire department. Civil society works when citizens take responsibility, in one way or another. For us, our small service has been to care for children in need of a temporary, loving home where children can find their feet, experience a measure of healing, and move on to a better future.

After thirty-three years, it is about time to retire, to pass the baton to others. We hope this book will inspire others to take up the challenge, and will provide those that do with some helpful tools to meet the task ahead.

In this book, we will argue that all children in care have been victims of violence in one way or another, and that the primary need of these children is loving nonviolent re-parenting. We have developed a model of caring for foster and adoptive children that does not resort to violence to produce obedience, change, or growth. In what follows we make explicit what we have learned and internalized in caring for children who have been victims of violence in the home.

We say "re-parenting" because the children we have cared for have already been parented—always inadequately and often abusively. These children need parenting again.

We say "nonviolent" because children who have been victims of violence need to experience a different way of living.

We say "loving," not in any sentimental way, but as we tap into a long tradition that has said that loving relationships are the *summum bonum*— the great good—of human life.

Our account is realistic. As Oliver Cromwell is reported to have said to artist Sir Peter Lely, "Paint me as I am, warts and all." We have attempted to do the same, and we "tell it as it is." In these pages you will find many warts. We tell the story as honestly as we can, mindful that our telling is from a particular perspective. Mostly, we have enjoyed our time as foster carers. Sometimes, we have wished we were doing anything other than foster care. We have experienced great heights of joy, and the meanest lows of despair. Though the rewards are many, we do not gloss over the difficulties foster carers face in welcoming strangers into their homes. This book is not about abuse, nor about sociological or psychological analysis—there are many excellent books that do that already—but rather about the experiences and reflections of foster carers who have developed a particular way of caring. Though we write primarily as foster carers, we write also as educators, writers, and academics. We both have advanced degrees. Andy teaches philosophy and is chair of the philosophy department in a state university. Jane works on a crisis support team for emotionally disturbed children and teenagers. We are white, middle class, British Americans.

Our hope is that our story will help people in different ways. We hope some will give at least a part of their lives to caring for the children of others—perhaps not for thirty years, but at least for a few. We hope that current foster carers who read this will be spurred on to keep up the good work they are doing. We hope that caseworkers and case managers might gain some insight into life inside a foster home on an everyday basis. We hope that carers, workers, and policy makers might look more carefully at nonviolence and adopt its goals and techniques in training foster carers.

What makes our practice of loving nonviolent re-parenting a useful addition to other literature and practice in the field is our emphasis on the kinds of re-parents we need to be. This is different to an emphasis on a set of rules to follow, or on techniques to employ (though both are important in different ways). Underlying our approach to caring for children is the work that Andy does in ethics. Moral philosophy is about how we ought to live. In ethics (moral philosophy and ethics are the same field) we have grown used to either rule-based ethics (after Immanuel Kant, 1724–1804, a German philosopher) or else to "the greatest good for the greatest number" (utilitarian ethics, after J. S. Mill, 1806–1873, a British philosopher). Since the 1980s, there has been a noticeable turn to an earlier view of ethics. When asked "how shall we live?" the answer given is that it is not merely by following rules, nor by thinking about the best outcome for the most people. The answer is about the kinds of people we should be. Simply put, better people make better decisions. Better people make for better communities. Better communities make for a better society. You can have all the rules in the world, but if you do not have decent people, the rules will not help at all. (This view has been termed Neo-Aristotelianism, after the ancient Greek philosopher Aristotle, 384–322 BCE.) We have taken this approach as foster carers. We have tried to apply this philosophy in our care of children. What are the characteristics of a good parent? What would someone who has taken on the task of caring for abused, maltreated, or neglected children look like—not physically, of course, but temperamentally! In this book, we focus not so much on rules or outcomes, but on how we can be the best foster carers we can be.

In other words, loving nonviolent re-parenting is as much about the development of re-parenting character traits as it is about the children we care for. This sounds, at first hearing, counterintuitive, as most of the literature, and certainly the current training of foster carers, emphasizes a "children first," and "the child's needs are foremost" approach. While this is of great importance, our assertion is that we can only care for the maltreated or abused child's needs when we have developed certain character traits that enable us to do so. Perhaps we should say rather, *have the intention* of becoming a certain kind of person characterized by certain character traits. Becoming a loving nonviolent person is a process that lasts a lifetime. None of us have truly "made it" in the sense of "having nothing left to learn." At best we are learning to walk a particular pathway. But, intention to do so is of paramount importance.

Traditionally, this type of philosophy centered on character traits (often known as virtue ethics) has focused on "happiness" as the goal. We place happiness in quotes because the traditional view of happiness is more than merely feeling happy. It connotes a life of well-being, "being well in doing well," philosopher Alasdair MacIntyre calls it. It is more expansive than just a feeling of happiness. Where we modify this philosophy is in saying that rather than the goal of becoming a happy person, we choose the goal of becoming a loving nonviolent person.

It is a subject Andy has written about extensively, but it is a philosophy we both consciously adopted in the early 1980s. Though the news media is full of the stories of violence, some scholars have begun to demonstrate that in terms of *actual* violence, western society is becoming increasingly nonviolent (see, e.g., Pinker 2012, whom we discuss later). Nonetheless, because of media portrayals of violence, and the deeply imbedded assumption that violence solves issues, nonviolence still seems counterintuitive. The common assumption is played out in the movies' "myth of redemptive violence." The myth tells of conflict between good and evil (the "good guys" and the "bad guys"). As the story progresses the bad guy becomes dominant, and carries out atrocities against the good. The audience is drawn empathically to support the good guy, while beginning to hate the bad guy. When the good guy is about to be completely overcome (and the audience is on the edge of their seats) the good guy manages one last violent assault on the evil. After one last death throe (just as you thought evil was beaten), through one last valiant and violent outburst, good finally wins. The audience feels good that evil is defeated, and knows once again that victory comes to the good person who uses violence against the bad. The story is played out in world affairs daily as governments of all stripes threaten the use of violence as a last resort. The media dutifully repeat the refrain in the news. The perennial cop show after the TV news tells the stories again. It is no wonder when nonviolence is first considered it seems counterintuitive!

Nonetheless, nonviolence is increasingly being applied to many areas of life. The witness of loving nonviolence is found in all the world's great traditions, though often a minority one. Like a golden thread running through the warp and woof of history, saints, sages, and mystics—from Loazi and Mozi in China, to Gautama Buddha in India, to Jesus of Nazareth in Palestine, to Leo Tolstoy, and the feminist ethicists of care in the modern world—loving nonviolence has been an important philosophy of life. Mahatma Gandhi (1962, 2001) and Martin Luther King Jr. (1986) exemplified the use of nonviolence in social justice and social change. Peter Ackerman and Jack Duvall (2000) document numerous social movements that effectively used nonviolent techniques to achieve great change. Marshall Rosenberg (2005a, 2005b) has written creatively on applying nonviolent communication in all aspects of personal and social relationships. However, as yet, nonviolence has not been specifically applied to re-parenting abused, neglected, and maltreated children. This we intend to do: to apply intentionally the theory and practice of loving nonviolence to the care of children.

This book, then, is a synthesis of:

a) Our practical experience in re-parenting;
b) Andy's academic work in ethics, and Jane's in the philosophy of education;
c) An intentional way of life that sees love and nonviolence as the greatest good.

This book is a personal reflection. We speak for no others than ourselves—though, briefly, at times for the children we have cared for and others like them, and perhaps, too, for foster carers who have faced similar dilemmas. Yet, we have no official position, no party line. While we are certified foster carers, we do not represent the County by which we are certified.

The book is part narrative and part theoretical looking at issues. In this way it is an exercise in theory and practice. Our practice of foster care led us to think deeply about what we do and how we might do it better. Our foster caring has been influenced by what we have begun to think about children, about love and nonviolence, and about the system. For us, theory and practice go hand in glove.

In terms of methodology, ours most closely approximates to the participant observer method of the anthropologists and sociologists, combined with a philosophical analysis. In participant observation studies the researcher becomes part of the group she is studying, to gain as deep an understanding as possible. How could one know what it feels like to be a foster carer if one has not had the experience? However, our research status is mostly after the event. We did not begin foster care in order to research foster care. We became foster carers to help meet a social need. It was only after many years of growth and development that we began more objectively to analyze the social function of the foster care system, and our role within it. The great strength of this methodology is that it allows the researcher to get a much deeper subjective understanding of the object of research.

A disadvantage is that it is usually a longitudinal study. It takes many years truly to integrate into a subculture. In our case, this was not an issue as we had thoroughly become "insiders" before we began to cast an objective glance. A further disadvantage is that because the sample size is small (the group the participant observer becomes a part of) it is difficult to draw general conclusions. However, the methodology is often suggestive for further quantitative studies. We hope this book will have that effect. A final disadvantage is that when the researcher "goes native," she tends to lose her objectivity. In our case, through our academic studies we have been able to draw back from the subjective experience of foster care to take a more objective viewpoint—at least to some extent.

Some of the stories we tell arose while we were foster carers in the United Kingdom (from 1982 to 1995). It is likely that procedures and best practices have changed since then. When we speak of our experiences in the United Kingdom, they reflect then current practices when we lived in England.

The situations we describe and stories we tell in this book are all true. We have changed details (gender, names, ages, and places) to provide anonymity, but only insofar as the change does not distort the issue we are speaking about.

1

Responding to a Major Need

I can hardly believe what I'm reading," Andy said, his voice slightly muffled from behind the broadsheet newspaper. "Have you read this piece on children in care?"

"Yes, I left it there for you to look at," Jane replied. She plucked toddler Ben off his Fisher Price first bike and placed him sidesaddle on her hip. "You're getting too big for this young man!" she said with a smile to the little boy. Then to Andy, "I had no idea. Three hundred children in care in our little town," pain now evident in her voice. "They say they are desperate for foster carers."

"There's a number to call to get information. What do you think?" Andy laid the newspaper down on the scratched pine table.

"I'd like to help, but the boys are still very young," Jane responded. "And the house is so small." And after a pause, "But, I don't think it would hurt to give them a call."

We both smiled. And so it began.

* * *

In 1982, according to a newspaper report at the time, in our little Pennine town in northwest England, three hundred children were in local authority care. There was a shortage of foster carers. In 2015, in our county in upstate New York, around 142 children are in care. Over thirty years later and 3,355 miles away, there is a shortage of foster carers here too. We have lost track of the number of times we have been called to see if we could take just one more child in an already full household. The situation is invariably "urgent," with a "desperate need." "There is no one else available," says the concerned family placement worker. The stories associated with the children are often heart-breaking. When all the beds in our home are taken, there is nothing we can do. The need is great.

However, we do not want to suggest that things are getting worse for children generally. Taken overall, in the developed world life has never been better for children. Since the Enlightenment and humanitarian revolution of the eighteenth century, and especially during the second half of the twentieth century into the twenty-first, violence against children has been in steady decline. Psychologist Steven Pinker compiles an impressive dataset from many studies that demonstrate how across virtually all historical measure of violence against children, children are better off now than ever before. He says:

> Though infanticide is the most extreme form of maltreatment of children, our cultural heritage tells of many others, including the sacrifice of children to the gods; the sale of children into slavery; marriage and religious servitude; the exploitation of children to clean chimneys and crawl through tunnels in coal mines; and the subjection of children to forms of corporal punishment that verge on or cross over into torture. (2012, 415)

Most children today do not suffer such egregious treatment at the hands of adults. Finkelhor and Jones showed how sexual abuse of children started to decline in the early 1990s (substantiations of sexual abuse were down forty-nine percent from 1990 to 2004, 2006, 685). Physical abuse substantiations also declined forty-three percent from 1992 to 2004, and juvenile homicide victims declined by fifty percent from 1993 to 2004 (Pinker 2012, 686). After 2004 rates have seen a modest decline (CTDB 2015, 3). However, the one area that did not show a decline was child neglect.

> Among maltreated children, the proportion reported as neglected increased from 49 percent in 1990 to 78 percent in 2009, while those reported as sexually abused declined from 17 to 10 percent, and the share reported as physically abused declined from 27 to 18 percent. The proportions have changed little since then. (CTDB 2015, 5)

It seems that most parents, nearly all the time, do a good job in caring for their birth children, and raising them to be decent members of society. However, a small percentage of parents do not, and their children are taken into the care of social services. Sadly, birth parents fail these children, often in their early years, and the damage done takes a long time to repair. In many cases, these children carry the results of their neglect and maltreatment into adulthood.

As a society we do not fail all children, but still we fail a great many. In 2013, there were across the United States 3.5 million allegations of child maltreatment involving 6.4 million children. Of those 3.5 million allegations 2.1 million received a Child Protective Services (CPS) investigation. Of those, 239,000 received foster care services, and 777,000 received in-home services (USDHHS 2015, xii). Sometimes, even with a grave suspicion that children are being mistreated, it is very difficult to find evidence. Though the level of evidence is less for taking a child into care than it is to prove abuse in a court of law, a mere suspicion of abuse or neglect is not enough. Some children who ought to be in Department of Social Services (DSS) care slip through the gaps. It is also the case that some children are hotlined where there is no abuse present. In New York State, the Child Protective Services Act, 1973, established a statewide central register of all reports of child abuse and maltreatment. The "hotline" receives calls twenty-four hours a day. Medical and hospital personnel, school officials, social service workers, childcare workers, residential care workers and volunteers, and law enforcement personnel are all mandated reporters. Sometimes, overanxious teachers, or neighbors, report perceived abuse, which is unsubstantiated. Still, the data reveal that after dismissing nearly two-thirds of allegations, over half a million cases of child neglect, maltreatment, or abuse remain each year.

When an allegation is substantiated, often the first intervention by DSS is to put in place services to help keep the children at home. If these preventative measures do not work, the child is often taken into DSS care and placed in a foster home, like the one we have provided for over thirty years (with a few short breaks to take a breath or two, cross an ocean and settle in a new culture).

Most of the children who come into care do so because of basic neglect (79.5 percent), physical abuse (18 percent), sexual abuse (9 percent), and psychological maltreatment (8.7 percent), usually at the hands of those who are their primary carers or their partners (USDHHS 2015, ii). Those neglectful or abusive parents are often the products of the same kind of abuse and neglect in their own childhood. The continuing cycle of deprivation, neglect, and abuse is relentless. In 2013, there were 1,484 child fatalities because of abuse and neglect in the United States, 2.04 deaths per 100,000 children (USDHHS 2015, 60). To put that in perspective, every two years in the United Sates parents or caregivers kill just about the same number of children as people who were killed by terrorists on September 11, 2001.

An encouraging sign is that according to the United States Children's Bureau, based on data submitted by states, numbers of children in care

3

have decreased from 523,000 in 2002, to 397,122 in 2014, while adoptions have remained somewhat static, from 51,000 in 2002 to 50,608 in 2013, with a peak of 57,000 in 2009 (USDHHS 2014, 2).

As a comparison to the United States, according to the United Kingdom Department for Children, Schools and Families there were 68,840 children were in the care of local authorities in March 2014 in England (BAAF 2015), including 51,340 in foster care (Statista 2015). This does not include children in Scotland, Wales, or Northern Ireland. In England there is one child in foster care for every 1,032 of the population. In the United States there is one child in foster care for every 803 of the population. Why there is what appears to be a significant difference is beyond the scope of this book. We note it only for comparison.

From our experience with the systems of both the United Kingdom and the United States it is clear that for every child taken into DSS care, there are several more who are "borderline." These borderline children face unbearable poverty, and often neglect, but do not face significant abuse. Often their parents are barely adequate, and just about provide the basic necessities. Some of these children are those for whom abuse seems obvious, yet which is difficult to prove.

Whatever we make of the data, it hides the incalculable suffering that children face in neglectful home situations, and the trauma of being taken into care. These half a million children need many tens of thousands of people willing to take them into their home to provide a safe and secure space to grow—at least for a while.

We have seen changes in both the United Kingdom and the United States. As we write, the United Kingdom system is facing a major shake-up, particularly with regard to adoption (led to a large extent by the *London Times* and its publication of the *Narey Report* in 2011). In the United States, the current vogue is for permanency and "concurrent planning" (see, e.g., Child Welfare Information Gateway 2012a). In both nations, the goal is to keep children in care for the minimum period of time, returning children to their birth parents or close family members, or else freeing the children for adoption.

Despite the great need for foster carers, and the many thousands of people who voluntarily put themselves forward to be trained (observed, and trained again) as foster carers, foster care has a very bad image.

This is especially so in the media. Over the years, we have taken an especial note of the way foster care is talked about in the printed and TV news, in books, and in everyday conversations. As we were writing this chapter, to test out our intuition we simply searched "foster care in the news" on the Internet. Near the top of the search results was this from CBS News in Texas. It was dated the same day we were writing:

> It will likely leave you with the strong feeling that the state of Texas owes these children . . . and perhaps thousands of other kids . . . a big apology. They are called this state's "Forgotten Children" . . . thousands of them in foster care . . . hidden from the public as they are taken from abusive homes . . . and moved elsewhere . . . over and over again. CBS 11 News gained exclusive access to records that, in incredible detail, tell the journey of three of those children—a boy, his sister and another child who would eventually become their brother. (Douglas 2012)

"Hidden from the public" sounds sinister, as if there is something to hide. In reality, "hidden from the public" most often means that loving foster families care for these children. This news story is typical of most. It neglects to tell of the many thousands of dedicated carers who day-in and day-out provide for children whose birth families cannot care for them. It forgets to tell, too, of the many thousands of children whose lives have been turned around by being cared for, who have returned successfully to their birth families, or who have gone on to successful adoptions.

"Children whose parents abuse them are taken into foster care," is a simple and true statement. The problem with the statement is that foster care is spoken of in the same breath as the abuse. Though foster care is more often than not part of an imperfect solution, a subliminal and psychological connection is made. In this way, in the popular media, foster care is presented as part of the problem. In the longer CBS report (above), the claim was made that the state of Texas moved one of these children eleven times, and that "no one loved him." The implication is that foster carers as a whole do not look after, nor love, the children in their care. This type of sensationalist reporting undermines and disrespects the essential work thousands of foster carers do.

Of the children in foster care fewer than one-half of one percent are further maltreated. According to the data, 320 children out of every 100,000 children suffer further neglect and abuse in foster care (half of whom are maltreated by their birth parents during visitation). This compares with 575 children taken into care out of every 100,000 children in the general population. These data mask the many children who suffer abuse in their birth homes who are not noticed by CPS.

(Throughout the book we use CPS in its American usage of Child Protective Services and not the British usage of Crown Prosecution Service.) This suggests that children in foster care are less likely to suffer neglect and abuse than children in the general population. This fact is very different to the media-influenced urban myth that children in foster care are poorly cared for; that foster homes are places of further neglect, mistreatment, or abuse.

Caring for abused children is a complex and difficult task. Children in foster care will often "try the patience of a saint." By the time children reach a foster home, in most cases the child has already known multiple abuses. To bring a measure of healing, to help turn the child around, is always an uphill task—in some cases an impossible one. Children in foster care are often so deeply damaged that no long-term solution can be presented other than keeping them safe. Nonetheless, the truth for most foster care is very different to the media portrayal.

To be sure foster carers are not perfect, but most foster carers are not villains. They make mistakes, like all parents do—like our parents did with us, and like we did with our birth children. While there is a minority of bad foster homes, for the most part foster carers are compassionate people who have seen a need in society, and are trying their best to help. Most become foster carers for very similar reasons we did: simply, they care and want to help. Most of the work of foster care is unsung, mundane, day-to-day caring for children. Foster carers take children whom others have neglected, abused, and failed.

Because of the grievous harm caused by violence that many have already received, it is imperative that foster carers exercise a very different approach to that which the children have known. The antidote for a life shaped by violence is not more violence, but rather nonviolence. It is the habits and virtues of nonviolence that this book is about.

We share a little of what it has been like to be foster carers. We suggest, too, what it is like for children to come into care with some of their presenting issues. We say "suggest" because we do not truly know what it feels like to be taken from parents and placed in a strange home. We tell the story from the perspective of watching and observing and talking to our foster children.

When we began as foster carers, we had been in our new home—a small two-bedroom, one-bathroom house provided by the church, where Andy was a trainee minister—for a little over a year. At the time, we had two of our three birth children, aged five and three. We had married young and were in our mid-twenties. Looking back, we had no idea where the journey would lead us.

The few months after our initial enquiry were busy ones: training courses, home inspections, references, and mountains of paperwork! At the time it seemed endless, but in reality it probably took about four to six months.

After the training and formalities, we were approved as foster carers and the wait began. When would we get the phone call to ask us to take a child? Would it be a boy or a girl? Would the phone call come in the middle of the day or during the night? Would we be able to cope? Would we be able to help the child entrusted to us? What if there is more than one? Had we prepared our own boys adequately for this stranger coming into our midst?

Then it happened: we got our first placement. It was a ten-month-old baby. We also got a real foster care shock! The baby came with a history. We had talked about hypothetical cases during training, but nothing had prepared us for the realization that the cases we had studied mirrored real people and real situations. We had half-wondered if we had been told extreme cases to make sure we were serious. The truth is, over the years we have cared for children from far worse backgrounds than the training prepared us for.

We were told that a young mother in mid-teens, had abandoned her baby. The reason? She wanted to spend a few days with her new boyfriend. He was also the father of the third child with whom she was currently pregnant. The young mother's mother (grandparent to our foster baby, and also quite young) was trapped in a spiral of prostitution, drug, and alcohol abuse. She could offer little help.

Thus we came across for the first time, and have met many times since, the cycle of neglect and, too often, abuse. Teenagers, who have suffered neglect and maltreatment, turn to other dysfunctional teenagers for love and comfort. The result is often an unplanned pregnancy. The young mother is often delighted. She is excited about the thought of something of her own to love. In some subcultures to become a mom, however young, is like a badge of office. This was how it was for her mom, and her mom before her. As often as not, the baby's father soon leaves the scene. The few who stay around to see the baby born are often quickly scared away from the responsibility of parenthood.

The reality of caring for a baby, especially with little money, no family support, and no job, is always different from the dream. It results often in stressed-out teenage mothers, babies who are neglected or maltreated, followed by intervention through CPS. The cycle continues to the next generation. We have cared for many children whose parents and grandparents were victims of neglect and maltreatment, and who spent time in foster care.

The mother of our first baby truly loved her child. She was just so young, and still a child herself. After committing to doing much hard work, and with social services' help, she was eventually able to have her child returned. We hope the story had a happy ending, and that our first baby had a good childhood and successfully moved into adulthood—it's hard to believe she will now be in her mid-thirties! Yet, we don't know the end of the story. That is often the case with foster caring. We are part of a child's life for a short time. Then they leave us and move on. Of course, some children do keep in touch, but many do not (more of that in a later chapter).

Since that first baby we have seen many more arrivals and goodbyes. We can remember almost all the children. In our memories they remain ageless. It is hard to imagine them as older, and impossible to visualize them as physically different than they were during the weeks, months, or years they spent with us.

The youngest child we ever took was six hours old. We picked him up from the hospital when his young mother walked out of the unit after giving birth. Andy thinks of it as the time he became a mother. We had been given notice that the teenage mom had agreed to give the child to adoption. We were still surprised when we received a call in the middle of the day to tell us that the baby had been born.

"Can you come straight away?" the flustered midwife asked Jane. "We are really busy and we can't spare anyone to care for him."

When we arrived at the major city hospital, we realized the truth of the midwife's words. The birth unit was in a state of barely organized chaos. A midwife rushed Jane into a room to sign papers. A second midwife thrust a bundle into Andy's arms and said, "I'm so glad you're here. This little one's not been fed yet. Here you go."

She handed Andy a bottle and left.

Andy looked down into the baby's eyes and there was an immediate bonding. The baby fed hungrily. Neither baby nor foster father took their eyes off each other.

For the next forty-eight hours Andy handled everything, barely letting Jane hold the baby.

"Hi Jane! It's Judy Smithwick, the baby's caseworker. Mum's changed her mind. She wants the baby back. We're just leaving now to pick him up." In those days, in the United Kingdom, a mother who voluntarily gave up her child for adoption had six months in which to change her mind. Babies were not placed with an adoptive family until after a six-week "cooling off" period, after which a change of mind was unusual. A foster family would care for the child during that time.

When Jane broke the news to Andy that the caseworker had called, he was heartbroken. The situation became worse when the young mother arrived, and blew cigarette smoke into the baby's little face as she picked him up.

Andy took the dog for a walk and cried for a while.

The eldest child we have cared for stayed until she was nearly twenty-one. She had a very rough start in life, then a turbulent transition to foster care. We witnessed many tantrums and violent episodes. Eventually she was able to settle and do well. She graduated from high school, went on to community college, and now has her own apartment and a good job.

But, in 1982, our experience of older children would be much later. We were still fairly new to foster care when we received a phone call asking us to take a ten-year-old girl. Our own children were still only three and five years old. Our first three children had been the same age or younger than our boys. A ten-year-old would be a whole new experience. Today, a ten-year-old seems like a small child to us, but then, a whole lot of questions arose.

"Andy, what time do you think we should put a ten-year-old to bed?" Jane asked.

"Jane, how much pocket money do you give a ten-year-old?" Andy also had questions.

"I'm not sure," Jane responded, "but I'm wondering do I need to help her wash her hair or should I leave her to do it herself?"

Of course, we soon resolved these questions with advice from friends, and cues from the child herself. But, there were other, unexpected side effects of taking an older child. It was our first experience with stealing.

* * *

"Hello, is that Jane, Susie's foster carer?" came the official sounding voice on the phone.

"Yes, can I help you?" Jane responded.

"I'm the head teacher of Susie's school. I wonder if you realize how much the school lunches cost?"

"Yes, I do. Is there a problem?"

"Well, you haven't been sending in enough money. You've only sent in fifty pence each week."

Jane was shocked, "No, we definitely gave Susie the full amount."

An agreement was quickly reached that we would pay by check in the future. (In the United States foster children receive free school meals, in the United Kingdom the cost of school meals is included in the daily allowance and foster carers pay for them.)

The head teacher continued the conversation and asked if we had missed anything else. We mentioned a few small items that we had just assumed we had misplaced including a watch. They were all found in Susie's desk.

2

The Multiple Violences Suffered by Children in Care

Most, if not all, children in foster care have been victims of violence. Violence might have been physical, sexual, emotional, or systemic. This is most often at the hands of birth parents or those associated with them. The literature on child maltreatment and abuse is extensive and is beyond dispute. We will not repeat the findings here. (See, e.g., foundational work by Finkelhor 1979, 1986; Finkelhor et al. 1983; Gerbner et al. 1980; Briere 1992.)

The child who has been beaten by his mother's boyfriend is a victim of violence. But so too is the girl who has been sexually abused by an uncle— as is the child who has been screamed at and called demeaning names. So too are the children who are taken from their mother, whom they love and depend on, to be placed into care. All of this violence against children is morally problematic. Something bad has happened to these children.

There might be one case of justification for some element of violence. When a child is taken into care because she is not safe at home, undoubtedly being taken from her mother is a violent wrench for the child. The violence of taking her away from her mother might be justified as the lesser of two evils. If the child remained in the birth home she might suffer further abuse. However, the abrupt tearing away from her mother is itself a violent action. It might be thought necessary, but that necessity does not lessen the violence.

Nonetheless, the question is: if children taken into care have already suffered so much violence, once in care should they suffer further violence? We became very clear early in our fostering career that to help repair the damage done through violence, we needed to provide not only a safe place away from violence, but also a loving nonviolent framework for children to heal and thrive. This is what this book is about: how positively to provide such a framework through a commitment to loving nonviolent re-parenting.

11

We need to explain what we mean by violence. The World Health Organization (WHO) has a working definition, adequate at least to begin a discussion:

> The intentional use of physical force or power, threatened or actual, against oneself, another person, or against a group or community, that either results in or has a high likelihood of resulting in injury, death, psychological harm, maldevelopment, or deprivation. (Grug et al. 2002, 5)

The WHO definition takes us only so far. It suffices as a definition of *physical* and *intentional* violence, but in foster care, as in life, we see types of violence excluded from the WHO definition. These other kinds of nonintentional and nonphysical violence need to be included.

Intentional, Foreseeable, and Accidental Violent Actions

According to the WHO, for an action to be counted as violence it must be intentional. In other words, the perpetrator of the action must intend to cause one or more of the several harms in the definition (injury, death, etc.). If a father intentionally wants to hurt his child and strikes him with his fist, that is violence. But what if the father is simply in a rage and lashes out, with no intention of causing injury? Is that, too, not violent? In other words, actions that are not intended to be harmful often have violent outcomes.

John is a teacher whose class is about to begin. He looks at the clock on the rear wall of the classroom and decides it is time to close the door. Recently, John's patience has been tested to the limit as Jason, an especially difficult and wearying student, has come late to class every day. As John is about to close the door, Jason ambles to the doorway. Something inside John snaps and he decides to "teach Jason a lesson." He slams the door hard just as Jason is about to enter. The door catches Jason hard in the face. His nose may be broken. It is very painful. At the subsequent disciplinary hearing, the school principal adjudges that the teacher had carried out an intentional violent action against the student.

But what if it didn't happen quite like that? As the class is about to start John goes to the door and begins to close it firmly. Jason, realizing that he is late again rushes toward the door. John does not see him coming and, sadly, the door crashes into Jason's face. His nose may well be broken. John is mortified! He did not intend to hurt Jason.

The school nurse records in her daily log that a student's nose was broken in an accident.

But what about one more different angle? This school is a very busy one. Students are often late. When students are moving between classes, it would be very unwise to firmly close a classroom door without taking particular care to ensure no student was trying to get into the classroom. At a meeting later in the day, the department chair offers teacher John a mild rebuke, "John surely you could have foreseen that your habit of closing the door with a bang would one day hurt a student!"

From teacher John's point of view, the three stories tell something different. In the first, John is intentionally violent toward student Jason. In the second, there is no violent intention. In the third, there is at least a hint of negligence, but no malicious intent. According to the WHO only the first was an act of violence.

However, from student Jason's point of view, each scenario produces the same result: a broken nose and a great deal of pain. Each scenario has a violent and harmful outcome.

The various harms that the WHO list may be caused intentionally, but also accidentally, and at times a harmful outcome might be foreseen, and hence might be avoided.

When we consider children in care who have suffered violence, we can't simply be concerned with those intentional acts of violence perpetrated by abusive parents. It is the violent effect on children in care in its totality that we need to address. Some violent harms will be caused by accident and some harms might have been foreseeable, and perhaps avoided. In working with birth parents, it is clear that caseworkers, therapists, and foster carers will need to address issues of intentional violence. But they will also need to address unintentional violence whether it is accidental or foreseeable.

Verbal Violence

Physical violence is clearly problematic. Yet, solely to focus on the physicality of violence misses those acts that are nonphysical in nature.

That harm is multifarious and not merely physical is clear. An abusive male may not lay a hand on his abused partner, but may make her life a living hell through the use of words (softly spoken or shouted), through insinuation, direct verbal assault, ridicule, and emotional blackmail. Verbal violence is clearly a form of mental and emotional torture. That

13

such a woman suffers harm is beyond dispute. Is the male's nonphysical harming a form of violence? We assert so.

* * *

Adrienne was a pretty, petite fourteen-year-old girl. Her smile lit up her whole face. The trouble was, the smile was rarely seen. She seemed to carry a weight far greater than her little shoulders could bear. When she came to us she was withdrawn to the point of being noncommunicative. Her academic scores revealed she was far below her actual grade level in all her subjects. Over time, as we gained her trust, Adrienne told her story. We pieced it together from the dribs and drabs of many little conversations and hints. She had been told she was "retarded" several times a day by her mother's abusive partner. So far as we could tell, she had never suffered physical violence. Yet, the deep wounds of emotional and psychological battering produced a deep harm. Emotional belittling, psychological assault is a form of violence that causes deep pain, as real as any physical assault. In Adrienne's time with us, with much care and affirmation from both the school and us, she was able to improve beyond anything we could imagine. She came out of herself. Her smile was more frequent. Her grades improved remarkably and she was able to graduate high school and move on with her life. Though her story had a happy ending, we realize the terrible harm caused by the violence of words.

* * *

The implication is clear for the care of children who suffer harm in multiple forms: psychological wounds are a form of violence. Simple neglect, too, where the child's basic needs are not met—food, adequate clothing, safe housing, and the like—is also a form of violence. We could argue that the WHO might mean this kind of violence in the notion of "power" threatened or actual that causes harm. The abusive parent intentionally uses his power to subject the child to harm. Psychological and emotional violence is, clearly, a misuse of power, and so may be implicitly included in the WHO definition. However, we would prefer to see it more explicitly stated.

* * *

Bill and George were six and nine. They were brought into foster care because of neglect. They arrived on our doorstep in the late afternoon, each clutching a small plastic bag containing their few clothes and treasured possessions. They were small for their ages, with dirty faces and unkempt hair. Their eyes opened wide as their glances darted everywhere taking in their new surroundings. They wore stained jeans that were a couple of sizes too small, covered by what would have been white t-shirts now graying, shapeless garments full of holes. Though neglect is often physical, it is also a form of emotional abuse. Bill and George had endured the taunts of peers about being smelly and wearing dirty clothes. They had been outcasts and friendless at school. Yet they had looked after themselves, eating whenever they could, as their parents succumbed to the ravages of substance abuse. After many months, as they began to trust us, we gradually built up a picture that included physical and sexual abuse and much emotional damage.

Structural Violence

A more subtle form of violence is structural in nature. It is one of the tragedies facing children in the care of social services. Often, the birth home is intolerable and CPS workers decide that the child must be removed. Yet, the removal itself is harmful to the child. In our society, we are just beginning to understand the very deep roots of attachment that form in the womb and in the first few years of life.

British psychologist and ethologist John Bowlby (1907–90) pioneered work on attachment theory. In the mid-twentieth century he published the *Attachment and Loss Trilogy*, which laid out the basis of a child's relationship with her mother. At the time, Bowlby's ideas cut across the post-Freudian understanding of childhood. His ideas have since been expanded upon and are now more or less taken for granted.

In brief, the kinds of attachment an infant makes in the early years of life have significant impact on the child's development and on how he forms relationships. A securely attached child tends to develop a better sense of self, be more independent, perform better at school, and develop good relationships with others. When an infant is neglected in those early months significant attachment issues may arise.

When a child is taken away from her birth mother in the first few months, those maternal attachment bonds are broken, or are not given time to form. The child suffers disorientation, emotional pain, and grief. Like any form of grief its usual accompaniments are shock, disbelief, anger, and depression. The harm done to the child's sense of self might be irrecoverable, or at the very least take a long time to repair. Children we see in foster care are often victims of such attachment difficulties.

Though Bowlby focused on maternal attachment, Michael Rutter challenged this in his *Maternal Deprivation Reassessed* (1981), based on clinical studies. Rutter modified Bowlby's theory by suggesting that children's attachment might not only be toward a mother, but toward a father or sibling. He further suggested that, whereas Bowlby said that attachment was to a single person, a child might attach to several people. Despite their differences both Bowlby and Rutter agreed that when significant attachment is disrupted in the early years, this is an indicator of later relational maladjustment.

Besides damage caused in the early years, some scholars suggest that attachment issues and harm caused can begin in the womb. (See, e.g., the collection of papers on prenatal attachment issues in the *Journal of Prenatal and Perinatal Psychology and Health*, December 2003.)

* * *

Sara was another preadoptive baby we picked up at only a few hours old. Her mother had discharged herself from the hospital immediately after giving birth. We knew we were going to care for her as soon as she was born, although we had not expected her to come to us quite so young. As we tended her during her first few days of life every now and then she gave a little cry that we could only describe as a frightened cry. These cries didn't last long, just a minute or so, and she was easily comforted. Was it our imagination, or somewhere deep inside herself did Sara know we weren't her mother or father? She was frightened and disoriented. Was there an instinctive sense of abandonment? We will never truly know. Interestingly, we did not experience this with other preadoptive babies who came to us at three or four days old.

* * *

Along with Juan's caseworker we were convinced that he had been physically abused. He had the tell-tale behavior of fearfulness, distrust, watching doors, and shrinking when Andy walked past. But when pressed, even gently so, by the caseworker Juan's response was, "What happens at home stays at home!" He repeated the phrase as would a well-drilled soldier who gives only name, rank, and serial number when questioned by the enemy. Sadly, we have heard that phrase many times since then. Once in the system many children in foster care are subject to an investigation, including invasive questions about their parents' behavior and lifestyle. Loyalties are tested. The system becomes adversarial as children are pitted against their birth parents. Attachments are tested, strained and sometimes broken beyond repair.

* * *

Ten-year-old Megan's mother really loved her. There was a strong attachment. Unfortunately, mom could not care for her adequately. Caseworkers at DSS had worked tirelessly over many months to keep Megan at home. The caseworker described the house as one of the dirtiest she had ever seen—excrement, human and animal in every room, old mattresses thrown on the floor of the bedrooms with no sheets to be seen, moldy food on unwashed plates that looked weeks old. Ultimately, they made the decision to remove her into a foster home. Megan arrived on our doorstep, a skinny, curly haired girl, in ill-fitting clothes, hair full of head lice.

Megan loved everything about foster care. She enjoyed having her own room, kept her possessions tidy, and told us constantly that she loved foster care. Yet, she loved her mother dearly. She was eager for her visits. She often phoned mom to tell her she loved her. It was clear that Megan suffered the inner turmoil of loving her mother, yet knowing that in many respects her life in foster care was better. During frequent conversations we were able to reassure her that it was good and right to love her mom, and that she could still do that, and like foster care.

* * *

When children are freed for adoption and eventually adopted, the adopters seeing their dreams of having children finally coming true, often change the child's name—most often surname, but sometimes first name too. It marks a new beginning. It says to the child, "Now you belong to our family." But, just as it marks a new beginning with the adoptive family it marks a distinct break with the birth family. Doubtless many adopted children make the transition well. Some do not. When attachments are broken, the child's ability to form attachments in the future is called into question. This too is a form of harm that derives from the system in which the child finds himself.

We are not saying that children should be left in an abusive situation where they face the prospects of further neglect and abuse. But we are saying that we must recognize that the system itself is a form of violence—not intentionally, often accidentally, but mostly foreseeable. The choice of taking a child into care might be considered the "lesser of two evils." Care might be better than the birth home, but is still not the ideal.

Four Loci of Violence

Based on what we have said so far we suggest four locations of violence that children in care face.

Violence in the Birth Home

The sight and experience of violence in the home enacted by caregivers and others traumatizes children even when they are not assaulted themselves (see Edwards 1989). For example, we have cared for a number of children who watched their carers systematically torture or kill their pets as a punishment.

* * *

Georgina had tight blond curls, dimples in her often-red cheeks and dark, almost black eyes. She liked playing with the assorted collection of dolls that she and the two other little girls in our home played with.

"Poor little Toby!" she said as if the words were coming from the doll in her hand.

"Has something happened to Toby?" Jane said, gently.

"Yes, poor Toby, poor Toby."

Jane didn't press the question. She had learned that children often will make a disclosure about some situation at home tangentially. But if the child is pushed, they will often clam up and the moment is lost. Often, in situations like this the child will simply move on. So Jane waited, apparently uninterested.

"Naughty Joe! Naughty Joe!" Georgina cried having the "Barbie" doll hit the "Ken" doll. "You shouldn't do that to poor Toby!" Suki, the Barbie doll, began to cry.

"What's wrong with Suki, Georgie?" Jane said. "Is she upset?"

"Yes she is. Very upset."

"Why's she upset?"

"Because Joe was a very bad man."

"What did Joe do?"

"He picked Toby up like this . . ." Georgina grabbed a soft toy from the pile and placed both hands around the neck of the toy, squeezing and shaking.

Georgina threw the stuffed toy to one side and continued her game with the dolls.

Georgina may have had a vivid imagination. Or, just maybe, she was playing out a scene of which she had been a part. A few days later, when Georgina's caseworker visited, Jane mentioned the game and the conversation.

"I just thought you ought to know about it," she concluded.

"Thanks! Poor kid! Unfortunately, your intuition is probably correct. Georgie's older brother has disclosed that last year mom's live-in boyfriend had strangled the kids' puppy in front of them. He did it as a punishment."

Georgina and her older brother were deeply scarred by the experience. Sadly, this was not an isolated experience and over the years we have cared for a number of children who had witnessed similar episodes of violence.

* * *

Beside the trauma of the event itself, many children also carry the guilt of having not been able to protect their siblings and pets more effectively against violence.

One child who lived with us was constantly worried about his mother being hurt in his absence. He felt his presence had lessened the beatings his mother received at the hands of her latest partner. Although only young he already saw himself in the role of protector. Another child worried that she had let her stepfather abuse her sister who was a year older and considerably bigger than she was. She never talked about the similar ill treatment she had received at his hands, only that of her big sister. We could easily see that there was no way she could have physically intervened. The stepfather was a big man and an eleven-year-old girl could not have prevented the abuse. However much we tried to explain and reassure her that she was not responsible, she still carried the weight of guilt that she had not tried to help her sister.

Removal from the Home, Placed in the System

We considered removal from the family home above as structural violence. We need to press in a little further. The system of foster care is a loci of violence in the nature of the system itself.

In everyday speech we use the word "violence" metaphorically. For example, we speak of the "violence of a tornado." There is no agency

19

behind the tornado with the intention of causing harm. Nonetheless, when someone says, "Did you feel that violent wind?" we know exactly what they mean. A kind of violence we see children in care subjected to is the violence of the system of care itself. Like the tornado, a system, or an agency, does not have intentionality of violence or harm. The system's agents may well be (and most often are) caring individuals whose only aim is the good of the child. Nonetheless, without intention harm is caused. Once again, the harm caused to children in this regard is multiple. It is no exaggeration to say that, often, children are ripped away—quite literally—from the arms of their birth parents, most often their birth mother.

Although in New York State it is the parent's legal right to see her child within fourteen days of the child being taken into protective services, the system does not always work perfectly. We know of instances where a child taken into care has not seen her mother again for weeks, or even months. In most cases this is because of parental nonattendance. In recent years, as laws have been tightened, this is thankfully now less the case than before. Parents now have to be informed about their rights and responsibilities.

Further, when a sibling group is taken into care, DSS will try to place the children in the same foster home. This is not always possible, especially with larger sibling groups. The separation from parents is compounded by separation from brothers and sisters. We have cared for children as young as six years old who have exercised the parental role for their younger siblings. In these cases, children suffer the compounded pain of losing what effectively was their baby. (The systemic violence of DSS is mirrored by the violence of the criminal justice system with regard to abused women. See, Edwards 1989, 153.)

* * *

Six young boys were taken into care. There was a large difference in age between the oldest and the youngest. DSS was only given a couple of hours notice that the children needed to be removed, and so was unable to place them as a sibling group. The two eldest were placed together, the two middle ones were kept together, and the youngest two were placed separately (although they were moved together within a few weeks when a space opened up in one of the homes). We were able to take the two middle boys. In the birth home, because of parental inadequacy, all four of the older children had assumed parental responsibility for the two preschoolers. They were grieving over the loss of their siblings, even with visitation rights. Although arrangements were made for visitation every two weeks, the parents often did not turn up. This was traumatic for all, even though the children saw each other. The situation was further complicated because there were two birth mothers, three birth fathers, and several step-parents involved. Although the children called each other brothers and had lived as such, actually two of them (full siblings) had no blood relationship to three of the others (two of whom were full siblings; the other had one parent in common with them).

* * *

The confusion, pain, guilt, shame, and terror that the child suffers is a clear case of harm. The action of taking children into care is, then, a violent action. In many cases, the child is taken into care because of other harms that the child is suffering. Even so, deep bonds are severed and the child is hurt further. In the short term, it may be that children need to be separated from the birth parents for a "cooling down" period, to be reunited fairly soon, under some kind of supervision. In the long term, it may be in the child's best interest to be separated permanently. Some parents cannot care for their children. Undoubtedly, even being separated from inadequate parents for good reasons, children suffer harm in the process. The child suffers the violence of separation. Neither the system, nor the caseworker acting within the rules and mores of the system, intends to cause harm to the child—quite the reverse.

This is the case, not only when the child is taken into care initially, but periodically as the system inexorably cranks through its bureaucratic motions. The child in care is a "marked child." We have observed many times that people make assumptions about both the child and her parents that make the child's life all the more difficult. People assume—and we have seen teachers, doctors, and, on occasion, even caseworkers make the assumption—that the child in care must be a bad child. She is watched in school more closely than other children. Parents of her friends are more reluctant to let their children play with her, or come over for a sleepover. It is the way the system works. It is systemic violence. It is often unintentional, but is violent nonetheless.

When we speak of the multiple violences children in care suffer, then, we include all those intentional physical assaults that cause harm, according to the WHO, but also those psychological and emotional assaults, together with the harm caused by the system itself.

Further Abuse in the Foster Home

Most foster carers we have met are good-natured, committed to children, and wanting to make a difference in the world. But not all are. Sadly, we have met, too, those who enter foster care thinking that foster care will provide a living wage. That is their motivation rather than care for children, and it can provide a conflict of interest. (In the United States foster care does not provide a salary, and we consider this in the addendum.)

Some foster carers, after many years of caring for very difficult children, face burnout and sometimes make wrong choices and bad decisions. For them, it is necessary to realize when the time has arrived to stop being foster carers, at least for a while. Doubtless, too, some are attracted to foster care because of the proximity to children. In this regard, foster care faces the same issues that any caring profession does that works with children.

Tragically, some children face further neglect, maltreatment, or abuse in the foster home. Studies are mixed. A 1994 study in Baltimore, looking at data provided by CPS from 1984 to 1988, suggested that foster families had over a threefold increased frequency of maltreatment reports as compared to nonfoster families. However, as we have noted, foster families are "in the spotlight" and many allegations prove unfounded. Most commonly, physical abuse was prevalent in residential settings while neglect was the issue for foster homes in the community (Benedict 1994).

A study in the United Kingdom, in 1999, looked retrospectively at 158 children in residential and foster care from 1990 to 1995 in the city of Leeds. There were 191 episodes of alleged physical and/or sexual abuse. Of those in foster care, foster carers perpetrated forty-one percent of incidents, birth parents on contact with the children twenty-three percent, and other children twenty percent. The report concluded that children in foster care were seven to eight times more likely to be assessed by a pediatrician for abuse than a child in the general population (Hobbes et al. 1999).

A more recent and extensive study in the northwest United States presented a different picture. The majority of foster children alumni reported positive experiences with their foster carers. Eighty-one percent expressed that they had felt loved while in care. However, almost a third reported some form of maltreatment during their time in foster care. This figure included both reported and substantiated claims of abuse. Substantiated rates of child maltreatment in foster care are very low, at 0.7 percent. If the reported, but not substantiated, cases were removed the overall percentage would be considerably lower. Nonetheless, the fact of further abuse in foster care is sufficient cause for concern (Pecora et al. 2005). It is in part why we wrote this book: to help foster carers and agencies discover loving, nonviolent caring, and perhaps, too, to provide better screening of foster carers and training opportunities in nonviolence.

False accusations are also a part of the picture. Foster carers are hotlined at a higher rate than the general public. According to CDHS, in the year 2000 out of a total of 230,000 allegations made against foster carers only 1,600 became reports of abuse and/or neglect (2014, 5–88). Some false allegations CDHS considers "naïve" when made by younger children who get confused between the past and the present, about what abuse is, or when fantasy is mixed with reality. Allegations are manipulative when the accusation by either birth parent or child is made in order to get what they want. Whatever the reason, when an allegation is made an investigation takes place.

* * *

John and Shirley were surprised by the early evening call by Lynn, a senior CPS worker. Shirley made light conversation as she made the coffee, her hands gently shaking as she poured water in the coffee-making machine. Visits from CPS are always ominous.

"I'm sorry to be the bearer of bad news," Lynn began as Shirley handed her the coffee mug. "There's no easy way to say this, so I'll get straight to the point. We have received an allegation of physical abuse of Alfonso. I'm afraid I need to see him."

Shirley turned pale. John, unusually stuck for words said quietly, "Of course. I'll get him."

Shirley and Lynn sat in awkward silence until John returned with the four-year-old.

"Hello Alfonso!" Lynn said cheerily. "I've not seen you for quite a while. Can I have a look at your hands?"

Alfonso held back, clinging to John's pant legs, and John gently ushered him toward Lynn.

She carefully unfolded his hands, and there on his right hand was bruising across the first joint of the middle three fingers, the skin broken on two.

"Ouch! I bet that hurt Alfonso. How did that happen?"
Alfonso looked sheepishly from Shirley to John.
"It's OK. Tell Lynn what happened," Shirley encouraged.
Turning back to Lynn, Alfonso said in a small voice, "Sally trapped my fingers in the door. She didn't mean to do it. She said she was sorry."
"I'm sure she was," Lynn said. "Now off you go, I want to talk to John and Shirley."
Alfonso scampered off while the three adults talked about the mishap, the trip to the doctor's for a quick checkup, the conclusion that nothing was broken, and the application of antibiotic ointment. It transpired that Alfonso's birth mother had seen his bruised hand, and assuming abuse had made a call to CPS.
"If only she'd asked!" Shirley said, with relief and some annoyance. "We could have told her what happened."

* * *

The reasons for the higher rate of hotlines on foster carers is easy to understand. Birth parents watch foster carers closely. Sometimes out of fear for their children's safety, and sometimes out of spite, jealousy or revenge birth parents will hotline a foster carer. Older children in foster care, too, sometimes make up stories about their carers. In training, facilitators make clear to new foster carers that the chances are that at some point, if they continue foster care for some time, there may be allegations and subsequent investigations. In John and Shirley's case, it was easy to demonstrate the cause of the bruising. It is not always as clean-cut. Children are forever falling over, bruising arms, knees, and heads. Mostly childhood mishaps are simply accepted for what they are. When carers are watched closely for any slipup, and in a culture where we are more acutely aware than ever before of the possibilities of abuse, foster carers live constantly with the reality of the hotline. According to CDHS, the odds are one-in-four that foster carers will receive a false allegation (CDHS 2014). For carers who are hotlined, there is often the additional worry that their own birth children may come under suspicion of neglect or abuse. To be questioned closely about parental care and treatment of children is a common accoutrement of being a foster carer.

We leave untouched accusations against carers that arise as a result of recovered memory therapy. In the 1980s and 1990s this controversial procedure was used extensively as the basis of finding sexual abuse that the client had buried in her unconscious. Recovered memory therapy is based on the idea that some traumatic events are so devastating that the conscious mind cannot deal with them. These traumas are buried in the unconscious, but, through various therapeutic techniques, may be recovered. The victim then relives the traumatic memory, and through some cathartic process finds relief and healing. The controversy is that before the therapy, the victim has no remembrance of the abuse. When recovered, there is generally no evidence of the abuse other than the recovered memory. It is also unproven why reliving a trauma, often extremely painfully, brings relief. At the very least, the theory is highly debatable, and though on the wane was very actively received for some time.

In our experience, none of the four agencies we worked with used recovered memory therapy with children in care, though we are aware of agencies that did. (Interested readers will find Ofshe and Watters, 1994, helpful in exploring and critiquing memory therapy.)

A General Culture of Violence

There is much cultural debate whether or not violence in the media affects children. Evidence is beginning to demonstrate that it does. Dave Grossman, former Army Ranger and sometime psychology professor at West Point, demonstrates that killing, rather than an innate disposition, has to be taught (1995, 2000). His main work relates to the training of soldiers to kill. Disturbingly, he shows that the methods used by the military to subvert the innate tendency against killing, are the very same methods used in video games. He says: "If we have reservations about the military's use of these mechanisms to ensure the survival and success of our soldiers in combat, then how much more so should we be concerned about the indiscriminate application of the same processes on our nation's children." (1995, 309)

According to the American Psychological Association, there are a number of studies from the 1960s onward that have demonstrated a clear negative effect on children who watch violence on TV. Children may become less sensitive to the pain and suffering of others. They may be more fearful of the world around them. Children may be more prone to use violence toward others.

> A 2010 review by psychologist Craig A. Anderson and others concluded that "the evidence strongly suggests that exposure to violent video games is a causal risk factor for increased aggressive behavior, aggressive cognition, and aggressive affect and for decreased empathy and prosocial behavior." (APA, "Violence in the Media")

Almost all the male children, and many of the female children, we have cared for in the last ten years have been drawn to violent video games. This includes very young children as well as teenagers. We have been worried when six-year-olds tell us the plots from mature rated horror films. We assumed their detailed explanations were correct as they were films we would not want to have viewed ourselves. It is possible that exposure to such games and TV will only affect a small percentage of the population. However, the mix of actual violence in the home with the virtual violence of games may have implications that we have not yet faced. There is at least a study to be done with regard to violence in the media and children who have been victims of violence.

Most of the violence children suffer derives from inadequate parenting. While we have worked with birth parents who are intentionally cruel, for the most part parents are violent because they know no other way to "care" for their children. In recent years, we have noticed an increase in children being in foster care because their primary carers are drug and alcohol addicts. One caseworker described it as an epidemic in our county. In 2013, almost twenty-six percent of child abuse was linked to drug and alcohol abuse (USDHHS 2015). Drug and alcohol abuse compounds the suffering of children.

There are no tests for parenting skills before a couple have a child. Parenting skills, if learned at all, often come by watching parents, aunts, brothers, and sisters with their own families. With the breakdown of extended families, suitable and stable role models are hard to come by. Often, when new parents reflect on their own upbringing they remember that parental discipline involves spanking and punishments, and so they do what they think is best. Out of principle or exasperation or frustration, they resort to violence. Often, part of the fostering task is to work with these parents, to model new ways of discipline.

3

Larger Houses, More Children

It is clear, then, that all children in foster care have suffered traumas as a result of some form of violence. Trauma results in multiple behavioral problems. These vary in intensity, but nevertheless can be distressing to both child and foster carer. For a child to come into foster care is scary. They are ripped from everything they have ever known. Even when the situation was abusive, the children often feel grief rather than relief.

* * *

Jane arrived at the DSS building. An hour ago she had received a phone call asking if we could take a brother and sister. In addition, could we drive to DSS to pick them up as they were part of a larger sibling group going to three different foster homes. Jane, who was last to arrive, found a crowd of adults and five scared children. She was introduced quickly to the two we were to take. The children looked at her, eyes wide open, clearly bewildered and terrified. They clung to each other. A few minutes later the caseworker announced briskly that it was time to leave. She knew, from previous experience, that long drawn-out emotional good-byes were not helpful to anyone. Jane led our two children to the car, talking all the while trying to put them at their ease. They still looked terrified. And no wonder! In the space of an hour they had lost all that was familiar to them, and placed in the hands of strangers.

* * *

The training courses try to give an insight into what it must feel like to be taken from your home. In New York, the Group Preparation and Selection/Model Approaches to Partnership and Parenting Course (GPS/Mapp) has an excellent exercise called "The Imaginary Journey."

The prospective foster carer/adopter is asked to think about their life, what they value, their possessions, their likes and dislikes, and their family relationships. A facilitator knocks (on the table) and says, "Hi, I'm the people mover. I want you to pack one case. You are being moved to a new home." The participant then is asked to reflect on what they would take, and what it feels like. The script is quite long, and those who take it seriously experience many different emotions. It doesn't mirror what children feel when taken into care, but it is a powerful exercise that begins to open emotional issues.

In the United Kingdom, we did exercises where we were blindfolded and had to trust strangers to guide us. We also had to let ourselves fall back, trusting that another would catch us. These are all useful exercises, and are helpful in preparation. They make quite an impression on upcoming foster carers. Yet, we know even those efforts can't come close to reflecting the depth of trauma experienced by the child.

Sometimes there is also separation from siblings. DSS caseworkers are committed to keeping siblings together. In addition to trying to keep siblings together, DSS try also to place children in a home where they can remain in the same school. It is often difficult. These are always two major considerations when placing a child. However, resources are thin, and the reality is that however desirable it is, neither of those things is always possible. The bottom line is: there are simply not enough foster carers.

We are writing this on a lovely, warm, sunny Friday afternoon in May. The writing has already been interrupted. Two phone calls, just a couple of hours apart, both asking if we can take another child. These were unrelated situations. Both were boys, one twelve and one fourteen. Unfortunately, at this time, we were only able to take one of them. Hopefully, the other found a home.

Children come into foster care for a variety of different reasons. In New York the categories are neglect; physical, emotional and/or sexual abuse; juvenile delinquent (JD); and person in need of supervision (PINS). A JD is a child who has committed a "crime," which is an offense (misdemeanor or felony) if committed by an adult. PINS is used to describe a young person with a pattern of behavior who comes to attention of the juvenile justice system, referred by parents, school, or the police. The majority of children we have had have either been placed in foster care through neglect, or through JD/PINS, which is a court-ordered route. Although many children are placed under the neglect category, as their stories unfold many have suffered physical, emotional, and/or sexual abuse as well.

* * *

It was only about eighteen months after our first placement that there were some changes in our family. The first, and most important, was that our beautiful third child, our daughter, was born. The second was that Andy's three-year placement as a trainee minister was coming to an end. We would be moving.

Our then foster child left us when Jane was six months pregnant. We decided we would not take any more children until we were settled in our new home. The location was still unknown, and life was uncertain for a while.

So it was a few months later, with two young boys and a baby, we left the small industrial town in the northwest of England for a lovely country village in the northeast. Andy was appointed as the minister of the local church. We moved into a four bedroomed church house. This appointment lasted for ten years, after which we came to the United States. Although when we came we did not expect to be here very long, here we remain. It is a long story and one we won't recount here. Suffice to say that Andy is now professor of philosophy and department chair at a college of the State University of New York, and Jane works in a school for emotionally disturbed children. In the United States we bought our own house, with five bedrooms and three bathrooms. Our houses in northeast England and in the United States have been convenient for foster care. Both changes of location required us to reregister as foster carers. Again, we did the mandatory training and started to open our home to children. Due to the larger size of our home we could take more children.

Often children still came singly, each child joining the others already in the home. However, we were now able to take sibling groups. When our own children were small, we often had three other children living with us. Now that our children are adults and have their own homes and families, we take up to six children usually over the age of twelve, though six at one time has been a rarity. We have never wanted to become a "children's home," with a certain institutionalization, but rather a family.

On several occasions we have taken sibling groups or part of a sibling group. The latter is usually when there are five or more children involved. We have been able to take two or three from the same birth family. These children face the additional anxiety of needing to know where their other siblings are, and if they are okay; especially when, as is often the case, older children have taken care of the toddlers and babies. Often, older siblings carry out parental tasks. When taken into care, it can be a relief not to have to do it. Yet, this new situation too comes with a grieving process.

Foster carers can do much to help alleviate some of the child's fears on that first day. We can't make any promises about when the children will see parents, or grandparents, or when the children will go home. Usually we don't know the answer to these questions. False promises don't help the children. However, we can assure them that we will try to find the answer to those questions.

We have always found that other children already in our home are excited about each new arrival. They are quick to make the newest child welcome. There is an affinity created through their mutual experience. The children within a household can become a great support for each other. This quick acceptance goes a long way toward helping a new child feel welcome.

A tour of the house is always a priority, especially showing the child where they will sleep. They need to know where toiletries are, which towel to use, where to put their clothes and treasures, even simple things like where the light switches are. The kitchen is, perhaps, the next most important room to show them around. Children need to know where the cups and glasses are, where the drinks are kept, whether they can just help themselves or need to ask first.

The first meal is always hard for a new child. We want to make it easy and comfortable. We now have a first meal routine that our current foster children know well. It has become something of a tradition in our family passed down from child to child over the years.

* * *

"Hey Armando, guess what?" shouted Lynn running down the driveway to meet the school bus.

"What up?" responded Armando.

"We're getting a new kid tonight," said Lynn excitedly.

"Word!" said Armando using "word" to express delight. "That means we get a sheet pizza for dinner." Like most teenagers he was always hungry.

Pizza is an easy first meal for everyone. We always assure new children that sometimes they may not like what we eat, but nobody is ever going to force them to eat anything, nor does anyone go to bed hungry.

* * *

We have had our fair share of difficult first days. Toddler Jimmy was handed to us as an emergency placement by an apologetic caseworker. The smell rising from the little body was horrendous. Everything he wore was saturated with urine and feces. Even his little shoes were sodden. Obviously he had been wet and soiled, dried and resaturated many times over. We needed to undress him quickly, wrap him in a big towel and put all the clothes and shoes outside to be dealt with later. The clothes could wait. He needed immediate care, bathing, and then feeding.

Other children have brought us additional, unplanned visitors. They came with head lice and, on two occasions, body lice. Truthfully, these are not very difficult to deal with. A bottle of lice shampoo is a must in the store cupboard of any foster carer. Yet, how awful for the child to know that their head needs treating on the first day in a new place! It is important to keep it lighthearted, not to allow the child to feel that they are unclean, or an outcast.

The children often arrive with little or no clothing. If they bring clothing it usually arrives in a black garbage bag or cardboard box. Foster carers do receive an initial clothing allowance to purchase new clothes if necessary. These can be administered in a variety of ways. In the four authorities we fostered for, the initial clothing allowance was handled differently. In one, a voucher was given to present to a specified store from which the clothes listed were provided. In another area, foster carers were given a lump sum even before the first placement. This was used to buy clothes, receipts were submitted, and the fund replenished. The full amount had to be returned when we stopped fostering. Our fourth experience was that a checklist is completed that shows the shortfall in the recommended wardrobe for a child within a certain age range. The money is then provided to purchase the additional clothing and shoes.

New clothes have to be provided on an ongoing basis, depending on how long a child stays with you. The shortest time a child stayed with us was only three days. In that case, clothing was not an issue. The longest placement was over six years. The initial clothing grant is used in the first season and foster children, like birth children, grow at a fast rate, outgrowing clothes usually before outwearing them. We have always made it a policy that our children do not look out of place among the other children their age. In an age of designer labels, this is quite expensive and the amount given to clothe the children is barely adequate.

These little strangers also come with a variety of habits. Many have never had cleanliness instilled into them. Regular showers and teeth cleaning are outside their experience. They can be clever in avoiding these daily habits.

* * *

Jane called twelve-year-old Mark to one side. "Mark, you have really been playing hard. Perhaps, you could go and have a shower now."

Mark answered, "Do I have to?"

"Yes you really do, you smell a bit sweaty," Jane insisted. "It's good to keep yourself clean and shower every day."

Jane heard the shower running. But only five minutes later Mark reappeared. His hair was dripping onto the clean shirt he'd been given to put on. It only took Jane a few seconds to realize that he hadn't showered. He had simply changed his shirt and put his head under the tap to wet the hair!

* * *

The shower issue can be quite difficult when dealing with teenagers. Many simply don't see the need for cleanliness. They are obviously too big for their foster carers to go into the bathroom to help show them how to bathe. Yet they have never learnt how. When our birth and foster children were young we taught them how to keep clean. At the time, we didn't realize what we were doing. It was just a normal parenting instinct, almost made into a game. Rubbing soap all over, making bubbles, playing with toys in the bath tub, closing eyes so hair can be rinsed easily—a bathing routine.

When a fifteen-year-old has to be taught how to do it, it's not so easy. The only way it can be done is with constant reminders and supplying some very nice scented body wash. Then, lots of compliments when the child looks clean and smells nice. However, sometimes it feels an uphill struggle. Showers are taken only because we insist. The value of keeping oneself clean has not been internalized.

Of course, not all the teenagers are like that. We have had our share of teenagers who are extremely conscious of their looks. They spend hours in the shower and in front of a mirror!

Caring for Your Own Children

We have been asked, from time to time, whether we considered the needs of our birth children when we became foster carers. Often, at the back of the questioner's mind is the thought that our birth children might not have been safe. Bringing "disturbed" children into the home would bring uncalculated and unforeseen dangers for our birth children. Surely, they would be influenced for the worse?

From our perspective—the reader would need to talk to our three grown children to find theirs—the benefits of foster care outweighed the drawbacks. Without a doubt, our children were introduced to family issues such as neglect, trauma, and abuse by their foster siblings. Was the experience damaging? We like to think on the whole not! Our children learned important life lessons in sharing, gratefulness, and compassion. They grew into fine generous and compassionate adults. One of our children became a caseworker with DSS and continues to care for children in the system.

Early in our fostering career we made a decision to keep our first-born son the eldest child in the family. It was in part instinct (it just seemed right) and in part pragmatic (we didn't know what to do with older children—we had not grown into them).

With hindsight our decision was a good one. We have observed new foster carers with little experience take on older children with some difficulty. Birth parents, by and large, grow in their parenting skills as their children develop. This is one of the reasons we try to encourage good parents we know to try foster care for at least a while. It takes years to develop good parenting skills. Most of us have our one, two, or several kids and when they reach adulthood we breathe a grateful sigh of relief, if we managed a half-decent job. But all those hard-earned skills then go to waste! Perhaps foster caring ought to be like national service where every competent parent uses their parenting skills in a community pool of caring for others!

We wanted our birth children also to know that they were our permanent family. We realized that their young minds might work out that as children came and went from our family that they might be next! So we established rituals to help them bond as a sibling group. We made much of birthdays and special meals out. When children left our care, we would do something special with our own three children to emphasize their uniqueness to us, and specialness to each other. When the children were young we established a tradition of a trip to the "Jiggery Pokery," a wonderful antiques and bric-a-brac store with its own tearooms and amazing sandwiches.

Christmas offered its challenges. In *Harry Potter and the Sorcerer's Stone* (*Philosopher's Stone* in its British edition) J. K. Rowling has Harry's cousin Dudley Dursley counting his birthday presents. Dudley counts thirty-seven presents, one less than the previous year. He throws a tantrum! Poor Harry never receives much of anything from his muggle uncle and aunt. We were not quite as extravagant as the Dursleys toward our own children, nor as mean toward the other children we cared for. But, the number of presents at Christmas was an issue. As far as we could we followed a "gift-equity plan." Our foster children received much the same as our own children. This was fine until the Christmas visit when foster children would return home with piles (literally) of cheap toys. As often as not the toys would break easily and often did not compare with the toys we gave as presents. But to our little ones a pile of toys is still a pile of toys!

Our household was often full. At one stage we had six children under the age of eleven. Our three foster children were a brother and sister aged six and seven, plus a four-year-old. All the children were excited, enjoying the countdown to Christmas, with their chocolate candy Advent calendars—one little piece of chocolate each morning. We had shopped well, determined to make it a memorable Christmas for the kids. Stacks of wrapped Christmas presents were hidden in our bedroom, ready for "Father Christmas" to deliver them. We reached Christmas Eve satisfied that all was done and we could relax and enjoy the holiday. Then the phone rang. It was a caseworker sounding very stressed.

"Josie and Alan's mother has just dropped a bagful of Christmas presents for them."

Jane was surprised. "But she said she was absolutely not getting the kids anything for Christmas! You asked her lots of times."

"I know, the thing is we can't deliver. All our staff finish work for Christmas shortly. Could you possibly come and get them?"

Jane sighed. There went the relaxing Christmas Eve afternoon. It was an hour drive from our home to the office where the presents were. When Jane arrived the receptionist on duty handed over a large, black garbage bag full of parcels.

This presented us with a problem. How could we make it seem that all the children had the same amount of parcels? It was not a problem with our older boys. They had come to appreciate value. But the younger children all wanted to open the same number of presents. For them, quantity not quality was the most important thing. Late into the night, Jane combined parcels, putting two or three together and wrapping as one. She took some presents already wrapped and split the contents. Finally, it was achieved! When Andy arrived back from officiating at the midnight Christmas Eve service, stockings were full and presents under the tree. Everyone had the same number of presents to unwrap.

Another challenge was which toys were to be shared and which ones were the "sole" possession of one of the children. It sounds trivial to us now, but to a five-year-old then?

"Mum, it's not fair! Teresa plays with all my Barbie's, but she won't let me touch the ones her mum gave her!"

As foster carers we recognized how important these little trinkets from home were. They were precious links to home, or else assurances that birth mom really did love the child. Yet, we wanted to encourage generosity and sharing.

We came up with the "drawer system." We kept it in place for many years and it was remarkably successful. We purchased a drawer to fit under each bed. These drawers were the bed's occupant's private space. The agreement was that no one would touch anything in the child's drawer (not even the adults). This was their personal space to keep their treasures.

All other toys were kept in tubs and on shelves and could be played with by anyone. Even so, the children knew to whom which toys in the general tubs belonged. This was important because when a child moved on, all her toys, bikes, clothes moved on too. Still, for the child to place a toy for general playing was a generous act, and we encouraged it.

4

Thinking Further about Violence

We suspect that most people most of the time consider violence a problem. It's likely too that most of us also have mixed feelings about whether violence is always wrong. For example, philosophers have often considered self-defense a natural right. That is, if you are violently attacked, you have justification for using violence in self-defense. Agreeing with the philosophers, most people would consider violence, at least limited violence in self-defense, as legitimate—just so long as the violence is proportional. In order to protect life, family, and property, the courts will likely accept a plea of self-defense even if you badly injure someone. The courts will be less sympathetic if you shoot the offender a dozen times, and then shoot his family in revenge. Gratuitous violence—violence just for the sake of it—most consider a very bad thing.

Beyond self-defense, the waters get a little murky. Is state sanctioned violence (that of the military, the police force, and the criminal justice system) always legitimate? Even those who answer positively—that state sanctioned violence is at times necessary—usually agree that such violence has to be within limits and for specific purposes. When a concerned citizen posts to YouTube a video of police officers gratuitously beating up a suspect on the city street, there is a public outcry. A spokesperson for the police department gives a televized interview carefully explaining why such violence "is not what my department is about. These officers were simply bad apples in a barrow-load of good ones. We are here to serve and protect." The officers, if identified, are ideally, though not routinely, disciplined. Sadly, as we write several high-profile cases have caused deep unease in American society. White police officers, caught on camera, killed unarmed Black men. Grand juries refused to indict the officers. Mass protests followed. Such public outcry is evidence that not all state sanctioned violence is acceptable.

Why is there an outcry, and why does the police department have to distance itself from the violence of its agents? Because we intuit that such violence is outside the permissible boundaries of the kinds of violence the police must occasionally use.

It is not always easy to determine how a population thinks about wars. Without doubt, when the United States went to war in Afghanistan and Iraq the majority of United States citizens supported the wars. Over time that support diminished greatly. However, whether or not one supports a particular war, when there are reports that a soldier has "gone rogue" and killed a number of civilians, people find such violence unacceptable. Even soldiers, who are trained to kill, can only exercise their lethal violence under certain carefully outlined conditions. Most nations recognizing this to be true have become signatories to the Geneva Conventions, which lay out carefully what is and what is not acceptable in a time of war. The international community accepts that there is such a thing as a "war crime." Though some violence is acceptable in war, not all violence is.

Since the 1970s, and in the United States more especially so since September 11, 2001, the western world has been conscientized to the wrongness of terrorism. Terrorist atrocities—nonstate sanctioned violence against the "innocent"—are rightly condemned. It is inappropriate violence.

Some argue that, on occasion, to do good may require the use of violence. In philosophy, this argument is sometimes known as the hypothetical of the "ticking time-bomb." It has had many depictions, but in its current form it is usually something like this: A suspected terrorist is apprehended. The terrorist knows where a bomb is hidden that will kill many people when detonated. To prevent this greater act of violence, the terrorist ought to be tortured, a lesser act of violence. If the terrorist under torture tells where the bomb is, then a greater good will have occurred, despite the evil of torture. If this is the case, then it is therefore acceptable to use violence (even extreme violence) because good will result. This type of argument was used for fire-bombing Japan in spring 1945, and then for the use of atomic bombs in the summer of the same year. Toward the end of the Second World War, many United States and Japanese soldiers were locked in terrible conflict in the Pacific Islands. To do good toward the American soldiers on the islands meant using extreme violence against Japanese cities, killing thousands of civilians. The destruction of the cities prompted the early end of the war, and so the saving of thousands of American servicemen.

So the argument goes. Many find the argument compelling: the greater good, at times, demands violence.

This general argument is used for the physical punishment of children. To paddle the child will in the long run produce good. Culturally, we frown on parental violence against children, but we are not sure whether spanking children by their parents is always wrong—or even whether spanking is a violent act at all. This is beginning to change and we consider this further in chapter nine below.

So, What Is Wrong with Violence?

What is wrong with anything seems at first an easy question. Easy questions usually have complex answers. Most people have some form of moral sense, and that from a very young age. Come Thanksgiving, slice the pumpkin pie unevenly and the six-year-old who received a smaller piece will cry with indignation, "That's not fair!" Fairness is a question of right and wrong. It shows that the little girl has a moral sense.

It's clear that the moral sense may be more or less developed. Moral sense will also differ between people. Take the controversial case of abortion as an example. It's not the case that either the "pro-life" or "pro-choice" side is moral while the other is not. Those who assert the right to life of the fetus have a strong moral sense. Those who assert the right of a woman to choose what happens to her own body, equally have a strong moral sense. Somehow, from somewhere, we all imbibe a moral sense that some acts are good and praiseworthy, while some acts are indefensible, morally wrong. From where do we get that moral sense?

Some have suggested that the moral sense is a God-given faculty, something like an inbuilt conscience. Whether that is true or not is not provable and depends largely on whether someone believes in God, and what they believe about God. Others have suggested that the moral sense is based on the natural faculty of intuition. Some things just seem right and some things do not. Both these answers do not help us in the case just considered of abortion. In that case people on both sides have a strong moral sense, which may or may not be God-given or an intuition. Nothing in either answer helps us determine between competing moral senses.

Here we need something extrinsic to either "God" or "nature"— something that will help us make judgments about which moral sense is better, and that might help us refine our own moral sense.

Two extrinsic factors might help: tradition and reason. Tradition is the long and complex development of culture in which ideas are tested and changed, and accepted, modified and rejected. Tradition is rarely static as there is always movement within a tradition as it grows, develops, and sometimes declines. In the western world we have a long tradition that has included ideas from the ancient Greeks, and Christianity, and secularism, and more recently from non-western traditions. In this tradition there has been a growing moral sense that violence is morally wrong. It has taken a very long time to reach this sense.

An important part of this tradition has become known as social contract theory, first verbalized by Thomas Hobbes (1588–1679), and later by John Locke (1632–1704), Jean-Jacques Rousseau (1712–1778), and more recently by John Rawls (1921–2002) of Harvard University. These philosophers suggested that civilized societies live under a contract whereby citizens give up some of their individual rights for the sake of the community's—the commonwealth's—good. One of those individual rights is the right to use violence. Under the social contract, citizens give that right to the police authorities internally and to the authorized military externally. In return the state, through its police force and military, protects the citizen. The social contract has been an important element in the limitation of violence.

The tradition has more than its fair share of violent atrocities, sometimes of unprecedented magnitude. Nonetheless, in the long term, the sense that violence is morally problematic has grown. We no longer have publicly accepted inquisitions where large crowds gathered to watch people "hung, drawn, and quartered." We have gradually replaced violent punishment in the criminal justice system, in the military, in prisons, and in schools, with more humane methods of control. We are becoming more sensitive to cruelty against animals. There is a long way to go still.

The second extrinsic factor is that of reason—thinking about, and coming up with justifications for or against violence, and providing good reasons for doing so.

In this regard, philosophers have identified basic ethical ideas or *prima facia* ethical beliefs that can be justified, and that may help form moral sense. A prima facie position is one that will hold true unless we can find very good reasons for not doing so. Four are commonly identified, though sometimes philosophers opt for more. The four are:

- Autonomy (respect for individual choices and community agreements)
- Non-harm (nonmaleficence)

- Justice (fairness, equality)
- Doing good (beneficence)

Most ethical schemes have these four in common. Actions are considered morally wrong when one or more of these basic ethical ideas are violated. It is easy to see how violence breaches these commonly held, bottom line ethical claims.

First, when a person commits a violent act, that act does not respect the integrity and autonomy of the other person. We tell our children that their bodies are their own, and that no one else can do things to their bodies. We have grown more and more used to the idea that what happens to "my body" is a personal choice. It is the thinking underlying the idea of the "right to choose." We call this idea "autonomy," a word that comes from two Greek ideas—*auto*, the self and *nomos*, rule. Autonomy is "self-rule." Violence is an action that ignores autonomy and removes the right to decide what happens to your own body.

Second, a violent act causes harm to the other person. The idea of "non-harm" has a very ancient ancestry in both eastern and western philosophy. The promise to "do no harm" is the first promise that physicians take in the Hippocratic Oath. The idea of nonharm has been the ethical foundation of medicine since the fifth century BCE. In the east, the idea of *ahimsa*, nonharm or nonviolence, has been a foundational idea in Hindu and Buddhist ideas for at least as long as nonharm in the western tradition. Violence, in its nature, causes harm and is a breach of the principle of nonmaleficence.

Third, violent acts are often unfair to the person against whom the violence is perpetrated. This might not be the case in some instances of violence (say in self-defense). Yet, broadly speaking violence against the "innocent" is unfair. Violence does not treat the other as an equal, with equal rights, but as a commodity—a thing—with which you can do as you like.

Fourthly, violence hardly ever does good. It might be that violence may prevent a greater act of violence from taking place. In this case violence might be considered "the lesser of two evils." But, that is some way from saying that "evil" is "good."

Note that it is not a requirement for the wrongness of violence that it violates all four of these four prima facie moral principles. It is sufficient to demonstrate that violence fails on at least one count.

Philosopher Barry Gan in *Violence and Nonviolence* highlights five myths of violence: The Myth of Physical Violence; The Myth of the Good

Guys and the Bad Guys; The Myth of Necessary Violence; The Myth of Effective Punishment; The Myth that Nonviolence is the Coward's Way Out (Gan 2013). Though Gan's book does not directly address violence against children, his five myths have clear implications for foster care.

We have already considered the "Myth of Physical Violence," that is, that violence is only ever physical in nature. Much of the violence against children is psychological and systemic.

The "Myth of the Good Guys and Bad Guys" makes clear distinctions between people, who fit into one of the categories. In terms of foster care we might term it the "Good Kids/Bad Kids" myth where children fit into one or the other category. Children in foster care are, of course, bad children. (Why else would they be in foster care?) Bad children need to be punished. Punishment as pain inflicted for wrongdoing is that which brings change. The tragedy is that, more often than not, children in foster care are not "bad" children. They are children who have suffered terribly at adult hands, and who sometimes react badly to life circumstances. Yet, once labeled "bad" these children suffer further pain as punishment is applied.

The "Myth of Necessary Violence" follows on closely. A cultural assumption is that at times the only resort left to parents is violence. Children need it, for not only is violence necessary, but the "Myth of Effective Punishment" tells us that violence against children works. Finally, parents who choose not to exercise violence are perceived as weak, as the "Myth that Nonviolence is the Coward's Way out" does its work. "Tough love" requires good parents to forego their empathic side to punish children for their own good.

Philosopher and social justice advocate, Todd May (2015) adds two further reasons why violence is morally wrong. He suggests that the first-order values of dignity and equality tell us violence is wrong. All human beings are intrinsically valued, he argues. That is, the value of each human being is not dependent on what function they perform—in philosophy called instrumental value—but rather on simply being a human person. This type of thinking in the western tradition derives from German philosopher Immanuel Kant. Kant argued that we ought never to treat a person merely as a means to an end, but as an end in themselves—known as the categorical imperative. Put simply, we don't use others for our own ends, or any other end. We treat others with respect and with dignity. This has become the basis for the whole human rights tradition in moral philosophy.

Rights protect dignity. One of those rights, and part of that human dignity, is the integrity of our own bodies. It is always morally wrong to infringe on the body of another. This is a basis for why physical violence is wrong. It takes away the freedom of the individual to choose what happens to their own body. From this general principle, it is easy to see that violence against children breaches this foundational principle of dignity. To neglect, maltreat, or abuse a child removes the child of her dignity.

May's second reason against violence is that all human beings are to be treated equally (again derived from Kant). Equality is a moral rather than natural value. In nature there is a great deal of inequality. The weak are unequal to the strong. The strong survive; the weak go under. Yet, in human society we have arrived at a first-order moral value that all human beings are to be treated equally—not because naturally all share the same attributes (such as gender, strength, or reasoning ability), but simply because all are human. Yet, our culture has always struggled with equality as a value. It is easy to point out the inequalities of patriarchy, racism, sexism, ableism, and classism. Slowly, but surely, we are overcoming these areas of inequality on the basis that each counts, simply by virtue of their humanity. But, we have been slow to value the equality of children. Equality is for adults only. Children, all too often, are still considered the property of adults. "That's my kid! I can do what I like with my own kid." And so children suffer the same fate as property and are not considered equal with adult human beings. Our culture has long since settled the wrongness of violence against adults. Corporal punishment was abandoned in the military, in the prisons, and in criminal justice generally. Yet, corporal punishment of children in schools is still legal in nineteen states in the United States. (Spanking children by parents is not illegal in any state of the union—more on this in chapter nine.)

A final argument against violence is that it simply does not work. At first this sounds counterintuitive. It seems clear that in some instances violence works. A bully on the school playground is tormenting a younger boy. An older boy sees it, approaches the bully and teaches him a lesson. He thumps him a few times and tells the bully if he ever bullies the younger boy again he will get worse. Violence works! Or else, the same bullied-youngster tells his mom. She gives him lessons in how to treat the bully. The next time the bully tries his tricks, the younger boy delivers a few swift kicks to the bully's shins and a punch to the face.

The bully knows not to mess with him again. Violence works! In the 1950s and 60s comics and newspapers often had a Charles Atlas cartoon advertisement selling his body-building system. The cartoon strip ran:

> Scene 1: Bully kicks sand into the face of skinny man and girlfriend.
> Skinny man: "Hey quit kicking sand in our faces!"
> Bully: "Listen here. I'd smash your face—only you're so skinny you might dry up and blow away."
> Skinny man: "The big bully! I'll get even some day."
> Girlfriend: "Oh don't let it bother you little boy!"
> Scene 2: Skinny man kicking a chair in anger.
> Skinny man: "Darn it! I'm sick of being a scarecrow! Charles Atlas says he can give me a REAL body. All right! I'll gamble a stamp and get his FREE book."
> Scene 3: Skinny man has become a mirror of Charles Atlas.
> Skinny man: "Boy it didn't take Atlas long to do this for me! What MUSCLES! That bully won't shove ME around again!"

According to the commercial violence will always deal with the bully on the beach, and Charles Atlas will show you how! However, University of California, Berkeley philosopher Michael Nagler in his book *The Search for A Nonviolent Future* gives us reason to question if violence truly works. He distinguishes between what "works" and what works. Though violence might "work" in the short term, fixing an immediate problem perhaps, in the long-term violence does not work. He says, "every time we use violence to solve a problem we send the signal that violence is the way to solve problems" (2004, 92). Violence against children sends out all the wrong signals to the child.

Taken together, then, the problem of violence generally is that it ignores autonomy, causes harm, is unfair, does not do good, is based on false myths, strips those against whom it is used of their essential human dignity and equality, and finally does not work in the long run. If we are to look for reasons why violence is morally wrong, here they are.

Our question is whether it is ever right or good to use violence against children, that is, to ignore their right to their own bodies and to cause them harm, to act grossly unfairly, to cease from doing good, to strip them of their dignity, and to treat them unequally. Our answer is a resounding "no." Even if violence at times might be justified as "the lesser of two evils"—as in self-defense—such does not count when we are considering violence against children.

Our personal position on violence is more thoroughgoing than the positions considered above. We do not think that violence can be morally justified in any circumstances, and we consider ourselves "nonviolentists." Philosopher Robert L. Holmes coined the term "nonviolentist" in his 1990 *Nonviolence in Theory and Practice*. He used the term to refer to those who have a principled commitment to nonviolence. He made a helpful distinction between a "pacifist" who in principle is against war, but not all violence, and a "nonviolentist," who in principle is against all violence, which includes war.

However, it is not necessary to agree with us completely. If the reader can agree with us that there is a prima facie argument that: (a) violence is to be limited to rare circumstances in order to prevent worse violence, and that (b) when used violence can only be exercised by certain authorized people—then there will be a major restraint on the permissible use of violence.

5

Why Re-parenting?

We have coined the phrase re-parenting to indicate that task, with its associated skills and character, required for the difficult job of taking children damaged by violence and "parenting them again." We make a clear distinction between our meaning and "re-parenting" as used in the psychological technique of transactional analysis. This refers to the re-parenting of the "inner child" and is a form of psychological analysis with associated therapies (see, e.g., Pollard 1987, Childs-Gowell 2000). To re-parent the neglected, maltreated, or abused child is to try to undo the damage caused by inadequate and violent parenting by the intentional approach of loving nonviolent "parenting again."

It seems clear that if children are born a "blank slate," they do not remain so for long. Much that has been "written" on children who come into care has a continuing and long-term effect on their growth into adulthood. When children experience violence at the hands of caregivers, much work needs to be done in re-parenting nonviolently.

The literature on child abuse is vast and growing constantly, and training courses are many that focus on the children for whom we care—and rightly so. Clearly, foster carers and adopters need to empathize with the child's predicament to get a feel for why they exhibit the behaviors they do. However, to date there is little emphasis on the kind of people that are needed to care for these deeply damaged children. Loving nonviolent re-parenting focuses on the kind of people we need to be in order to care.

No single model is adequate for an understanding of the re-parental task. To help us we have taken clues from feminist philosopher Sara Ruddick, from psychologist Abraham Maslow, and from the current work being done on empathy by social thinker Jeremy Rifkin and others.

Mother's "Caring Labor" and Re-parenting

In 1989, feminist philosopher Sara Ruddick wrote *Maternal Thinking*—a groundbreaking book on the nature of mothering. Ruddick's book is in part a critique of the dominant ideals of masculine rationality. Women—mothers—have always practiced the "particularity, passionate attachment, and bodily engagement expressed in mothering" (p. x). This motherly practice has often been contrasted with the rationality of public life. Historically, the public sphere has been the domain of males, and the domestic that of females. Women have carried out the task of caring for children. The social construction of mothering, then, has been of the nurturer, carer involved in the day-to-day life of children. The social construction of fathering has been that of distant provider, the one who enters the child's life only sporadically. As it goes with the gender divide, the masculine task has been elevated and the feminine task deprecated, but often sentimentalized.

Ruddick uses Louise Kapp Howe's 1975 *Pink Collar Workers* to make the point clear. Howe reports a government study that rated work in terms of complexity. Jobs deal with data, people, and things. Each category was assigned a number measuring complexity. The lower the number, the greater is the complexity. A surgeon, for example, traditionally a male job, ranked the highest with a score of 101. (In a study carried out by the American College of Surgeons, still only twenty-one percent of active surgeons in the United States were female, 2010, 24). Traditionally female jobs ranked low—nursery school teacher 878; practical nurse 878. A foster mother's job also ranked 878. Here is a description given in the study:

> [She] rears children in her own home as members of family. Oversees activities, regulating diet, recreation, rest periods, and sleeping time. Instructs children in good personal health and habits. Bathes, dresses and undresses young children. Washes and irons clothing. Accompanies children on outings and walks. Takes disciplinary action when children misbehave. (Ruddick, 33)

As Ruddick comments, "If maternal work were as easy as this contemptuous description of it suggests, anyone could do it" (Ruddick, 33). Parenting has been considered a low skill task. Howe, Ruddick, and we disagree! To parent well requires immense skill. But, what neither the Pink Collar study nor Ruddick account for are the added complexities re-parents face in the difficult task of caring for deeply damaged children. But, the point is well made that the "caring labor" of mothering has been largely denigrated in our culture. It is precisely this generally denigrated labor that foster carers are called upon to do.

As Ruddick expands her thesis, she suggests three essential areas of mothering: protection (preservative love); nurturance (fostering growth); and training (a work of conscience). These summarize not only the work of mothering, but the work of re-parenting, and interestingly in that order. When a child comes into foster care the very first task is to protect; to provide a place where the various harms caused will no longer continue. The second task is to nurture, to care, to ensure that the child's physical, emotional, and relational needs are met (see below). The third task is to train, and in most cases to retrain, in many of the basic aspects of self-control and connectedness.

What Ruddick calls "mothering" we are calling "re-parenting" in the context of caring for children in foster care. Does this mean that only mothers can be foster carers? Are men excluded? Inasmuch as the task of re-parenting is much the same as Ruddick's description of mothering, then foster dads become mothers too! Most of the work we do with children can be encompassed in Ruddick's account of protection, nurturing and training. Society has changed, of course, and in general many males are performing more childcare (traditional mothering) and we are the better for it.

We have always considered part of Andy's task as a re-parent is to model a different way of being male than most of our children have experienced before. Many of our children have only known men as distant, or addicted, or temporary, or abusive to their mothers, or uncaring. Not a few children have taken some time to adjust to a different kind of male in their lives—at first deeply suspicious and sometimes afraid of all men. The truth is, this different way of being a male looks suspiciously like being a mother!

* * *

Katie was a blond, blue-eyed three-year-old. Coming from an abusive home life, Katie was terrified of everyone, especially men. If Andy entered a room she scooted to the other side of the room to find a corner. She had developed a habit of nervously twirling between her fingers whatever was close by, all the while staring wide-eyed at Andy. She remained hyper-vigilant whenever he was around.

We chose to let her be, always talking to her gently, but hoping that in time she would overcome her fears. A few weeks after she arrived we took a trip to the local shopping mall to buy the children new shoes for the start of school. As usual, we told the children to stay close, as we didn't want anyone to get lost. Quite out of the blue, Andy felt a small hand slide into his. He looked down and smiled when he saw it was Katie. A small triumph!

A Needs-based Approach

In answering the question: "what does it mean to be a re-parent?" we have found it helpful to use the formative work of Abraham Maslow (1908–1970), well-known for giving to the world a motivational psychology summarized as a hierarchy of needs. Simply put, he developed a motivational theory that showed how certain needs have to be fulfilled for a human being to reach their full potential. A chart of the hierarchy is generally presented as a pyramid with, from the base upward, physiological needs, safety needs, belonging needs, self-esteem needs, and self-actualizing needs—each level of needs building on the ones below. When one need is satisfied, humans tend to seek fulfillment for the next need, each level of need being more sophisticated than the ones below it. Lower-level needs are satisfied before higher-level needs. Abraham's original paper has now achieved canonical status, and like the canon in all fields is open to interpretation in a number of different ways. Agreeing with him that the human person is motivated by basic needs, our preference is to view those needs as a series of interwoven circles rather than a hierarchy—each need being met concurrently as we develop through childhood and continue into adulthood.

These basic needs continue through all of life. To be a parent is to help the child meet those basic needs through loving care and example. When a child first comes into care her immediate needs of safety, physiological issues, belonging, and esteem are met concurrently. Self-actualization is, perhaps, a need to be met later in life. We look briefly at these needs and their relevance in re-parenting children in foster care.

Physiological Needs

Maslow's first level of need (one of our bundle of needs) is physiological. To re-parent meeting a child's physiological needs is to work directly against the violence they have suffered. Much of the damage children in care have faced has been physical in nature. Much of our work is providing a safe place where the child comes to learn that they will not

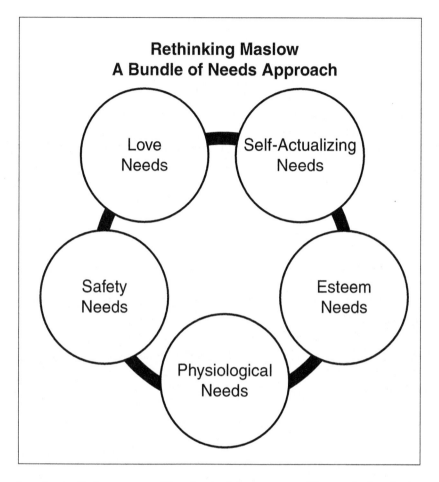

**Rethinking Maslow
A Bundle of Needs Approach**

- Love Needs
- Self-Actualizing Needs
- Safety Needs
- Esteem Needs
- Physiological Needs

be physically hurt, nor suffer physical deprivation. This includes clothing, sleeping space, warmth, and freedom from the fear of being hit.

Quite obviously one of the major physiological needs is that of food. Many of our children have not had this need met adequately, and children have not been fed enough. For them regular meals have been a rarity. The child has no confidence that he will be fed again. A food-deprived baby we cared for used to scream and scream when she finished her bottle. We knew to give her more would have been harmful. Even at only a few weeks old the baby's behavior reflected fearfulness that she would go hungry. This little girl left our home at eighteen months old to go to a lovely adoptive family, who had been unable to conceive a second child. At the time she left she still had problems with food. If anyone left a drink or food on the table she would grab for it and try to eat or drink. She had to be carefully monitored. It showed us that harm done in the first few weeks had long-term effects.

Recall the WHO definition of violence as the intentional use of power "that either results in or has a high likelihood of resulting in injury, death, psychological harm, maldevelopment, or deprivation." When a parent or guardian deliberately refuses to give food to a child, that is a form of violence.

Equally, we have cared for children who have been poorly fed, but overfed. These children equally suffer as their overweight size causes health issues, affects their ability to exercise, and is a foundation for future bad eating habits. In these cases the re-parenting task is to help moderate food intake, and to ensure that foods eaten are healthy. One young man who came to us severely overweight lost over forty pounds in his first nine months—not through "dieting" but simply through regular, healthy eating and more exercise than he was used to.

We have cared for many children with eating disorders, and were surprised in the early days just how many children suffered in this way. Finding old food hidden in the bedroom is a common part of a foster carer's life! Food is comfort. Hidden food is an assurance that there is something to eat if there is a need—just in case.

* * *

"George, do you know what I found this morning in your bedroom?" Jane said gently. A number of times, she had found food hidden in George's bedroom, often that had become bad and moldy. For a while she let it go, but after some weeks decided to broach the subject with him.

The somewhat scrawny eight-year-old looked down at his feet.

"I'm not cross with you George. I just want to chat about it," Jane continued, putting an arm around him reassuringly.

She continued to coax him until George was able to talk about it.

"But, what if the food runs out?" he finally blurted out.

"We always go and buy some more!" Jane said lightheartedly. "Haven't you been with me every week to the supermarket. We buy lots of food. There'll always be food for you George."

Despite the reassurances, the problem persisted. Jane decided to tackle the issue more proactively. She told George that she would give him a snack in a little bag each night to put near his pillow. It would be there if he woke up and was hungry. It became a nightly routine.

The bag was packed with a few animal crackers, or some carrot sticks. George went to bed happily.

With his new sense of food security, the food hoarding stopped. The food in the bag each night was rarely touched. George didn't really want food; he wanted security. Before he came to us, many nights he had gone to bed hungry. He had gone to school the next day still hungry.

Even after George had stopped hoarding, Jane continued to put the little bags of food next to his pillow.

"Jane, I don't think I want a bag of cookies tonight," George said, a few months later.

"Why's that Georgie?" Jane responded, a little surprised, but quite relieved.

"Don't need them," George said, sloping off out of the kitchen. Jane put the little plastic bag back in the drawer. The food hoarding was a thing of the past. George's need of physiological security had been met.

Safety Needs

Almost all the children we have cared for have not had their safety needs met. Most have been placed in foster care because the adults in their lives have failed to keep them safe.

Even so, we are often amazed at the resilience of young children. Stevie, who had lived with us for several months, was to be allowed home for unsupervised visits for a few hours each week. Stevie was eight, a big boy for his age, but we were concerned about safety and asked him if he felt safe going home. His reply was, "Yes! I'm OK. I check the trash can, and if it is full of bottles [alcohol] I make sure there is always a door between me and my mother so I can run out." Although this boy had tried to develop strategies to keep safe, it should have been the adult providing a safe home. Like Stevie, many of our children have told us stories of how unsafe home life had been. Open drug use, child and spousal violence, and prostitution have been common. Young children trying to protect mom from an abusive boyfriend is also frequent.

* * *

Angel had settled well and played well with our other children. Initial reports from school were good, and we had high hopes of being able to help him. However, we noticed that Angel was especially on edge around bedtime. He was anxious and unsettled and would resort to pacing. He was not sleeping well. Clearly, something was bothering him, but he would not say what it was.

As was our practice, we did not push Angel to tell us. Opportunity would naturally arise and we waited for that moment. We continued to build trust, fairly sure that he would share with us in his own good time. Eventually his story came out. Angel was worried about his mom. Her partner was physically and verbally abusive, and the repeated occurrence happened before bed. Angel had taken on the parental role of protector. He felt that he was the only person who could keep his mom safe. On a couple of occasions he had even called the police. If he had not been there, who would be able to do that? So, he worried and he paced. Might his mom be injured, or even killed?

We tried to reassure Angel that the authorities were doing their best to keep mom safe. We are not sure he believed us. His pacing continued. We are not sure we believed it ourselves. Women with abusive partners are extraordinarily vulnerable. On more than one supervised visit with mom, we noticed new bruises. She told the caseworker she had tripped. The caseworker could not protect her, any more than Angel could. Our reassurances to Angel were somewhat hollow. We could not keep his mom safe. What we could do was provide a safe place for Angel. Sometimes that is the only thing foster care can do.

Love Needs

It seems obvious that one of a child's basic needs is the need to be loved, and most birth parents really love their children. However, sometimes the tangible form of love, the way the parent expresses love, is skewed. We have coined a phrase to describe these children: "utterly spoiled, utterly neglected." Not only are the child's attachment and belonging needs neglected, but she will often experience the trauma of violent rejection. When love is expressed, it is often expressed as the giving of material goods. One fourteen-year-old showed us an old scar, and told us that the parent had hit her with a sharp object. Then the girl described with glee the stuff she had bought as the parent had tried to rectify the violent attack with presents and cash. We have experienced many teenagers who have learned to "play the system," and have not grown out of tantrums, demanding things when at the store, at school, or at home. When their tantrum becomes unbearable, their parent punishes, often violently, feels remorse afterward, and spends more money on the child.

Esteem Needs

Many of the children who have passed through our care have very low self-esteem. They often feel worthless. They have very little confidence in anything they are or do—teenage girls who spend hours looking in the mirror, constantly asking for reassurance that they look okay. Though common in teenage years, what we have seen in abused teens is an anxiety about themselves that goes beyond the normal. Frequently told growing up how useless, or ugly, or pathetic they are, these children have never had their need for esteem met.

When children first arrive, our priority (after food) is usually to clothe them. The few clothes they bring are mostly unwashed, don't match, and are either too small or too large. If we wouldn't have sent our own children to school in those clothes, then we won't send children in foster care. The first trip to the mall is to find at least sufficient clothes to send the child to school. However, it is not as easy as it might seem. Children who have been deprived are often overwhelmed by the choices available at Gap, Target, American Eagle, and T.J. Maxx. To choose has never been a possibility. Faced with choice, children simply shut down, become morose, and withdraw. It takes time to rebuild a child's self-esteem.

Much of the rebuilding involves words that build up a child rather than belittles and tears down. It is a long-term process. From experience, for many people one cruel and harsh remark can tear down the works of scores of kind remarks. When a child has known only cruel words, the rebuilding of esteem requires much patience and much repetition of kind speech.

Self-Actualizing Needs

Self-actualization is at the top of Maslow's hierarchy. The implication is that only after other layers of need have been met, does one become self-actualized. The self-actualized person is one who is self-fulfilled, who is becoming everything she is capable of becoming. This might be considered the goal, the achievement of purpose. In a very real sense, it would seem futile speaking of self-actualization when a child is hungry, afraid, feeling unsafe, and starved of love. The task of foster care is to provide all of those needs. Self-actualization follows when basic needs are met. However, it's not the case that self-actualization *cannot* take place until all those needs are met. It is just more unusual. In our experience, when a child settles, having had his immediate needs met, the child begins to experience at least the beginnings of self-fulfillment.

But it is a long process. As often as not, we are happy simply to meet a child's basic needs and to keep her safe.

Maslow's need-based approach is a good starting point for the parental task. In re-parenting the task of the foster carer, or adopter, is to see that the child's physiological, safety, love, esteem, and self-actualizing needs, which have not been met by their birth parents, are met. The goal is to help the child become a well-balanced member of society.

Human Nature?

Much ink has been spilled about what human nature is, or even whether there is such a thing as human nature! The answer we give to the question is more than merely academic. Any intervention in the lives of children will be most effective if it is in line with the way children are. By and large, scholars have wrestled with the thoughts of the three great philosophers of the modern world who tried to answer the question of human nature. We met these thinkers in chapter four. Most other thinkers tend to fall in line with one of these three, or else synthesize their positions.

Thomas Hobbes suggested that human nature was pretty bad. He is perhaps most remembered for his memorable view of humanity expressed as, "solitary, poor, nasty, brutish, and short." He believed that the natural state of human beings was one of war of all against all. Like many in his day he espoused the idea of human depravity (an idea based in part on a certain reading of the Bible, and in part on observation and experience). Left to their own devices human beings would do terrible things. Because this was so, Hobbes suggested that the primary need among humans is control of the lower animalistic drives. The bottom line is that human beings are born bad and need to be trained to be good.

John Locke modified Hobbes' position. Locke was not as pessimistic about human nature, and he popularized the idea of the *tabula rasa* or the blank slate. He said a child was, "only as white Paper or Wax, to be moulded and fashioned as one pleases" (Pinker 2012, 432). Human beings are born neither good nor bad. By and large most people, most of the time, naturally tend toward the good, respecting each other, and each other's natural rights. Nonetheless, people do have a propensity to go off the rails and to disrespect the rights of others. A civil society will help keep people on the right track.

Jean-Jacques Rousseau reacted strongly against Hobbes and followed Locke with the idea of human nature as a *tabula rasa*, terming it an original innocence (contra the Christian view at the time of original sin). Like Locke he thought that human nature tended toward the good. But unlike Locke, Rousseau was quite pessimistic about society. It is society, he thought, that makes people turn bad. If human beings still lived in a primitive state, without the trappings of "civilization," we would all be better off. Whereas Locke thought civil society a general good and protector of natural rights, Rousseau saw society as providing chains. Although people are born free, because of the influence of society, everyone, everywhere, is in chains.

It's easy to see the influence of these philosophers on the way our culture has viewed children and how to care for them. Hobbes gives us the idea that children need strict discipline. Without it they run wild. Kids must be tamed! Locke helps us see that children are born like "blank slates," but tend toward goodness. If we simply provide a good civil environment children will do fine. Rousseau would warn us that though children tend toward goodness with the right kind of care, they need protecting from the corrupting influences of society.

These three positions are incompatible—at least Hobbes's is with Locke and Rousseau. Nonetheless, the Hobbesian view of human nature has had a lasting and profound effect on how parenting has been viewed in western culture. In Hobbes's view there are no redeeming features of natural human beings. Like a wild animal the natural human will must be broken. Views like this were a large part of the problem of European colonialism and imperialism. When white Europeans "discovered" other lands, the inhabitants were perceived to be in a state of nature. Such nature has to be broken, or else eradicated. The history of colonialism is a shameful history of breaking and exterminating indigenous peoples.

In the Hobbesian worldview, children are born in a "state of nature" that he conceived as brutal and harsh, a war of all against all. Much education, until reforms in the twentieth century, was based around a harsh regimen designed to tame and control the wildness of children. Parenting in part, too, was about breaking the spirit of a child, to make the child civilized. As an example, consider the words of Susannah Wesley (1669–1742), mother of the founders of Methodism, John (1703–1791) and Charles Wesley (1707–1778):

> When they turned a year-old (and some before) they were taught to fear the rod, and to cry softly. By this means they escaped abundance of correction they might otherwise have had. That most odious noise of the crying of children, was rarely heard in the house. The family usually lived in as much quietness, as if there had not been a child among them. . . .

In order to shape the minds of children, the first thing to be done is to conquer their will and bring them to an obedient spirit. To inform the understanding is a work of time, and must with children, proceed by slow degrees, as they are able to bear it. But the subjecting the will, is a thing which must be done at once and the sooner the better. For by neglecting timely correction they will be overcome with stubbornness, and obstinacy. This is hardly ever conquered later and never without using such severity as would be as painful to me as to the child.

(In a letter to John Wesley dated July 24, 1732. 1997, 370–371)

Wesley's view was not uncommon. Breaking a child's will more often than not included corporal punishment and the infliction of pain. Such views of parenting remain a shadow in the background for many parents today.

* * *

Scotty was pretty wild, and one of our first children. He was used to being out on the streets until late at night, sometimes staying out the whole night. After school finished, when he chose to go to school, he did as he liked. Bedtimes, baths, regular meals, and school attendance were all new to him. Old habits die hard, and he frequently "left school" without telling anyone where he was going. We had to deal with the worry of where he was, followed by phone calls to DSS after he was absent more than the agreed upon time. Each time he went missing his birth family were notified. His father used to call us with the advice, "Beat him! Don't just talk to him. Beat it out of him." We never followed his advice.

* * *

Though many parents, and re-parents, do not know this background philosophy on human nature, they are familiar with the struggles between differing views. Our culture gives mixed signals: at one time insisting on more discipline, punishment, and control, and at another time sending a message of individual rights for each child. Negotiating between these positions is difficult for parents.

However, a fourth view of human nature, especially as it relates to morality, was suggested during the Scottish Enlightenment by Philosophers David Hume (1711–1776) and Adam Smith (1723–1790). These philosophers suggested that moral sense derives from the innate human ability to sympathize with others. Though they used the word "sympathy," they used it more in the sense of empathy—being able to feel with others in some way, to know something of their feelings. It is because we feel for others that we begin to shape our values about the correct behaviors toward others. Morality is based, then, not on reasons but on feelings. Hume famously suggested that reason (what we think about things) ought to be a slave of the passions (what we feel about things). For both Hume and Smith, human beings—other things being equal—lean toward empathy for others.

Recently, something similar to this fourth view of human nature has been suggested by a number of scholars and popularized by Jeremy Rifkin in his *The Empathic Civilization*. He says in the introduction to his book (in error, as this view of human nature is an ancient one):

> A radical new view of human nature is emerging in the biological and cognitive sciences and creating controversy in intellectual circles, the business community, and government. Recent discoveries in brain science and child development are forcing us to rethink the long-held belief that human beings are, by nature, aggressive, materialistic, utilitarian, and self-interested. The dawning realization that we are a fundamentally empathic species has profound and far-reaching consequences for society. (2009, 1)

Perhaps of most interest for our purposes is a consideration of how human beings develop empathy. Rifkin analyzes recent research to suggest that empathy in part derives from "mirror neurons." Briefly, and simplistically, he suggests mirror neurons are a function of the brain that develops in early childhood to enable the child to feel for others—to put himself in their shoes, so to speak. The human brain, it seems, is not fully "hardwired" at birth, but develops during the early years. Essential to the development of mirror neurons is loving care. Rifkin says, "In other words, parental and community nurture of infants is essential to trigger mirror neurons' circuitry and establish empathic pathways in the brain" (Rifkin 2009, 86). He, summarizes research in this way, "When a child feels he is not loved as a person or that his love is not accepted, his maturation stalls, and he begins to develop aberrant relationships and express pathological symptoms, including aggression, obsession, paranoia, and hysterical and phobic behavior" (Rifkin 2009, 58). Rifkin's use of mirror neurons is important, but not quite correct. It is not the case that mirror neurons only produce an empathic response in children. According to Harvard psychologist Steven Pinker:

> The problem with building a better world through empathy, in the sense of . . . mirror neurons, is that it cannot be counted on to trigger the kind of empathy we want, namely sympathetic concern for others' well-being. Sympathy is endogenous, an effect rather than a cause of how people relate to each other. Depending on how the beholder conceives of a relationship, their response to another person's pain may be empathic, neutral, or even counterempathic. (Pinker 2012, 578)

Children are clearly mimics, and it is necessary for children to be around adults who demonstrate sympathetic concern for others. Our challenge with children in care is that too often they have lacked such adult empathic concern and behavior to imitate. The debate about mirror neurons and how much weight we can place on them will doubtless continue.

However, Rifkin's analysis with regard to empathy does not stand or fall on mirror neurons alone. He uses child psychology to suggest that children develop "five modes of empathic arousal" (Rifkin 2009, 110). The first three are automatic and mostly involuntary: motor mimicry, classical conditioning, and association with a victim of pain based on the child's own experience of pain. Two higher cognitive levels are role-taking and perspective-taking. In this way the child associates with the victim's distress, and allows the child to imagine how the other feels. Rifkin suggests that much of a child's empathic development depends on the way a child is disciplined in the early years. "It is in the disciplining experience that children develop a keen sense of empathic expression" (Rifkin 2009, 117). He says further, "Obviously, inflicting corporal punishment on the child for a social transgression is likely to have the opposite effect and make the youngster less empathic in the future."

Primatologist Frans de Waal lends weight to this renewed emphasis on empathy using evolutionary biology. He provides ample evidence that many animals, including humans, exhibit empathy quite naturally. He says, "the traits produced by natural section are rich and varied and include social tendencies far more conducive to optimism than generally assumed" (2009, 45). Nature, it seems, does not select for the most aggressive. The fittest for survival have often been those whose social sense (empathic sense) is most developed. But like the other authors we have considered, de Waal recognizes that human beings have the potential for both empathy and aggression. He says humans are "bipolar apes" (203).

What these authors help us see is that the view of human nature as always aggressive, and naturally violent, is incorrect. Given the right circumstances and environment human beings have immense capacity to cultivate empathy.

If this fourth view of human nature is true—that children will naturally tend toward empathic concern rather than aggression under caring conditions—it has profound implications for foster care and adoption. On the one hand, the behaviors we see in children, who have been victims of violence, are not because of any innate badness. Rather, it is a lack of adequate and loving care in the early years. On the other hand, this analysis lends weight to our concern that the task of foster carers and adopters is to try to turn around that lack in early life through loving nonviolent re-parenting.

Empathy and Self-Control, Example and Presence

Despite this positive analysis of human nature, we are not freed from a consideration of the more problematic aspects of human behavior. There is potentiality in human beings for both good and bad. Even if we reject (as we do) the Hobbesian determinist view of human nature as thoroughly bad, we must still deal with the consequences of disrupted empathic growth in the early years of childhood. Part of the success of a well-lived life is to be able to control the baser elements of the human psyche (anger, jealousy, hate, and such) and to develop the higher faculties (love, kindness, sympathy, and such), and we need to do so in a society governed by civility and respect for others. A large part of the re-parental task, then, is to help a child learn self-control and to develop empathy. Rifkin says:

> The extent to which empathetic consciousness develops, broadens, and deepens during childhood, adolescence, and adulthood, depends on early parenting behavior—which psychologists call attachment—as well as the values and worldview of the culture one is embedded in and the potential exposure to others. (Rifkin 2009, 9)

In a normal loving environment these tasks are part and parcel of family life. It is common for a child to be jealous of a younger sibling. Caring parents take care to ensure that the toddler is loved as much as the newborn. When children face neglect, maltreatment and abuse, self-control and empathy are in short supply. If a child does not learn self-control in childhood, the chances are that he will become a mal-adjusted and troublesome adult. To develop a child's innate empathic side—her feeling for others, the ability to place herself in their shoes—nurtures her immense potential for love and compassion. The empathic, self-controlled adult is the good citizen. We have often seen this lack of self-control and empathy expressed in the phrase "I don't care!"

"I don't care about you, or anyone else" is a lack of empathy; "I don't care what I do" is a lack of self-control. If we had a dollar for every time a foster child has said, "I don't care!" we could take early retirement!

* * *

Jane's silenced mobile phone vibrated in her pocket for what felt like the hundredth time that day. Our latest foster child, sixteen-year-old Debbie, had been with us about four weeks. She loved to send text messages and we were beginning to regret lending her the hundred plus dollars to get a new phone. She was paying us back from her weekly check from her first ever part-time job at a local store.

"Jane, I'm hungry. Can we go out to McDonalds?"

"No I'm making dinner," Jane texted back.

"But, I'm hungry. Can you drive out and get me Subway? Just me you don't need to get the other kids any."

"No. When I buy food out, it will be for everyone, not just one person."

"I don't care about them. [The other three children] I'm hungry!"

* * *

Re-parenting then, besides being about Ruddick's protection, nurturance and training, and Maslow's helping to meet the child's needs that were inadequately met in the birth home, is also about providing a model of empathy and self-control. In order to model this for our children, we have found that it is necessary to be a certain kind of presence in the home. If we expect our children to develop empathy and learn to control their urges and desires, we must first let them see what it looks like. We do our best to live out what we hope the children will grow toward.

This requires a certain diligence for the re-parent. It means that we exercise care in speech, tone, reactions, mannerisms, and ways of dealing with conflict. We teach empathy by being empathic. We teach self-control by being self-controlled. As the children note everything we do and say, we need constancy in every area of life. It's a tough call!

6

Teens, Tantrums, Sex, and Substance Abuse

As every parent knows all too well, the preteen years are over all too quickly. As our children got older so did the foster children in our home. Fostering teenagers can be both rewarding and frustrating, and most acknowledge that the teenage years can be difficult. Childhood is being left behind. Young people are trying to move toward maturity and find their own place in an adult world. As we have seen, scholars of child behavior generally agree that the more secure a child's attachments and roots are, the easier this transition to adulthood will be. Many of the teenagers we have cared for are doing well. Several, now in their twenties and thirties as we write, are at university or working. Some even have their own families and are successfully rearing their own children. Many keep in touch with us by an occasional phone call, text, or email. Facebook has proved useful in following many of the important events in some of their lives.

Sadly, a few of the teens we cared for served prison sentences for misdemeanors. Their lives are still a turbulent ride taking them to who knows where. Some of our girls became pregnant far too young, and their babies, too, were taken into care—although to date no one has become pregnant while living with us!

Graduations, Proms, and Suits

We have sat in many overly warm auditoriums watching these young men and women graduate from high school. For many it was such an achievement after months or years working in close partnership with the schools to finish in a decent time. One girl was especially pleased, as she was the first in her family for many generations to graduate from high school. Proud biological grandparents and aunts attended the ceremony with us. They, too, were delighted at this young woman's success. They all returned to our home for a celebration party. Together, the birth and foster families, were applauding the achievement of this young person.

* * *

"I'm not going to the prom. I'll feel stupid," announced Tyler.

"We're okay with that," replied Jane. "We know you don't like big crowds. Give it some serious thought and let us know if you change your mind. You only leave high school once."

Several other conversations followed this one. Tyler alternately decided to go, then changed his mind and did not want to attend. Some days it felt like he changed on the hour! Finally he was firm, unwavering, he definitely wasn't attending. A couple more weeks passed by, during which the subject wasn't mentioned.

"Jane," Tyler excitedly burst through the door, "My teacher is hiring a limo for all the kids in our program to drive to the prom."

"Tyler, it's tomorrow night!" Jane answered, incredulity in her voice.

"I know but the teacher asked, and I can still get a ticket if I take the money in the morning," Tyler said.

"But what will you wear? You can't go to the prom in jeans," Jane responded.

Tyler's face dropped, "I hadn't thought of that. Can't I just hire a tux?"

A quick phone call to the shop from where most of the teenagers hire their tuxes for the prom confirmed our fears. It was too late. All the orders had to be in the week before. Undeterred, we headed with Tyler to the mall, rushing around various stores trying to find the right clothes. We managed to equip him for the prom—tux, shirt, bowtie—right down to new shiny, black shoes, at considerably higher cost than hiring from the school prom supplier! But, Tyler looked great the evening of the prom. We took many photographs as he climbed into the limo with his classmates.

When he left us, he also left "the suit" as it has become known. He claimed he would never wear it again and didn't want it. It is still in new condition, but has proved useful on a few other occasions.

While writing this chapter Jane received a text message. It was from another young man who was now at college while working and living independently. He had been with us for a number of years and had made a good transition. "Can I borrow 'the suit," he said. "I've got an interview and I need to wear one." Of course, the answer was yes!

Fostering teenagers is a bit like riding a rollercoaster—or, at least how we would imagine a rollercoaster ride as neither of us have ridden one! The ups and downs of fostering teens are daily, even hourly. Sometimes joys and crises happen at the same moment in different lives. At the very least we can say, there is never a dull moment!

At the same time that we were running around the mall looking for Tyler's shirt, suit, and shoes, Jane was interrupted by a phone call. It was from home.

"Hello," said Jane, "What's the matter?"

"The police are here," said Katie, sounding a little scared, "They want to talk to Brandon, but he doesn't know what he should do."

"Let me talk to the trooper," Jane replied.

In the ensuing conversation Jane ascertained that Brandon had hit someone at school, severely enough that the other boy's parents had sought medical attention. They were pressing charges. The police cannot interview children in foster care without the presence of their attorney or caseworker. The state trooper was very understanding, and we agreed that we would contact the child's caseworker the next morning so that an interview with Brandon could be arranged. Still, the phone conversation took quite a while. Then Jane had to calm Katie down and talk to Brandon, who was very worried. Then we returned to suit shopping for the Prom the next day. All in a day's foster care!

Suspensions and Disruptions

In Brandon's instance, the school had imposed their own consequences. He was suspended for five days. As far as the school was concerned, the problem was solved for a week, and justice was served. In reality, school suspensions do little good for the child and cause headaches for foster carers, and we have always found them one of the hardest things to deal with. Our own birth children sailed through high school without a single suspension between them. With many of the children in foster care, out of school suspensions are commonplace. The trauma they have experienced causes behavioral issues. These tend to manifest at school in fighting, skipped classes, smoking where and when they shouldn't, and generally disruptive behavior. In our opinion, suspension tends to be self-defeating. In many cases, the teens do not want to be in school. When the school suspends them, the children welcome the days out. In addition, children in foster care, having been rejected already many times in their short lives, are rejected again.

For foster carers, one of the problems suspension brings is supervision. If a single carer, or both carers, work outside the home, as we do, it raises the major issue of supervision. Although many of the teenagers could be home alone, it is not advisable. A long lie-in followed by watching television or playing video games is, in our opinion, not desirable for someone who should be in school. How we have handled suspensions is dependent on the age of the teenager. A seventeen-year-old boy we can send down to the library with his schoolbooks ostensibly to study. If a tutor is provided they will meet him at the library. In almost every case, the teen asks can they have money to go to a fast food restaurant for lunch. We always say no! A lunch can be packed and taken, we do not want anyone to go hungry, but nor do we want it to be a fun day out. Of course, if the suspended child is only thirteen (or even younger) we have to handle it differently. We cannot send them to the library to study. They need to be home, often with an adult. This means missed days at work for us.

Over the years, we have had much experience with teens getting suspended. We still have not found a really satisfactory way of dealing with it. We understand that the chaos of their lives, and the trauma they have experienced, are the underlying causes. Yet, while we understand the behavior, we can't reward or ignore it. To reward such behavior does not help the teen mature and grow into adulthood. Soon she will have to learn to work with supervisors and colleagues. Developing those simple habits of getting on with people, and not reacting violently, or having a meltdown, begin in the school setting.

On a couple of occasions we have sadly had to tell DSS that we can no longer provide a home for a particular teenager. When a thirteen-year-old has fourteen days of suspension, usually three or four days at a time over a two-month period, it becomes too disruptive within the household. We cannot take that many days off work, we cannot pay for childcare for extended periods, especially as it is usually clear that the situation will not be improving in the next few months. In such cases, it's possible that other foster carers, who are in the home during the day, might meet the child's needs better. Still, prolonged absences from school are not helpful in the long term.

Work and Money Issues

It is a sad reality that often, even by mid-teens, a child's ways are set and the course of his life is already determined. Sometimes we have had to realize that a particular teenager is too damaged for foster care. Some children need twenty-four hour supervision in a specialized residential setting. This is usually when the child has hurt someone, or pulled a weapon with the threat of violence of a more extreme kind. This type of situation is too unsafe for a home setting. This has only happened a few times. It is sad to think that because of early treatment a child is so damaged, that she remains a victim who is suffering.

In many ways the needs of teenagers are not much different from younger children. Teens still need discipline, food, exercise, and sleep. Yet above all they need their foster carers to be "parents," not their best friends. That sounds simple, but it is essential. Most children need structure and routine. While we do not set bed times for older teens, we do have quiet times after which everyone is expected to be in their own room with the house quiet. Music is allowed, but only with headphones.

Perhaps our greatest hope with many of the teens we have fostered is that we have planted a tiny seed. A different way has been shown to them. There does not need to be violence and chaos in their lives. Often the teens visit a few years later and we can see that they have imbibed something of what we have been teaching and modeling.

One thing that really helps to boost a teenager's self-esteem is finding an appropriate job. In our community there is specific help for teens over fourteen to provide life skills, among other things. This includes helping them find employment. Help is available through different organizations to achieve this. Funding pays minimum wage while the youngsters work within the community. Our teens have worked at the SPCA cleaning pens, walking dogs, and playing with cats, at the YMCA in both childcare and afterschool programs, in nursing homes and childcare facilities and, on occasion, in local stores as checkout assistants and general help. Many of these schemes are time limited and when they come to an end, on more than one occasion the employer has offered a continuing job to the young person. However, some of our teens have preferred to find employment themselves, with our help with the application process. These jobs are mostly in local stores or fast food places. As with everything else some of the teenagers do really well at employment and some don't. The main reason positions are lost is through poor attendance. They simply don't turn up for work if they don't feel like it. There is no sense of responsibility. Still, the majority of teenagers we have had do well in their positions. One young woman kept the same job in a local store through her last years of high school, through college and when she eventually moved to another state was transferred to another branch of that chain.

Employment gives the teenagers a lot of extra money—after all teens in foster care have clothing—a major expense—provided for them. We try to instill in them a sense of saving. We suggest that they open two bank accounts and put half of every paycheck in their savings account, keeping the checking account for spending. Although a couple of our teens have been diligent in saving, the majority of them spend all their money on electronics and entertainment. Most have no thought of saving for the future.

This is double edged. On the one hand for a teenager to have a job builds self-esteem. On the other, some of our children have earned around a hundred dollars a week. When all their needs are met by the foster care allowance (housing, food, clothes, and all essentials) it means they have a hundred dollars a week to spend on themselves. This is a very large amount. As things stand at present, as the teenager earns the money, he can do with it as he wishes. In our opinion, this is a flaw in the system. We would prefer that an amount the teenager earns would be given back to DSS to help cover the cost of their care; or better still, put the money into a savings account for when the child reaches eighteen or twenty-one. Such a system would still give the teen a sense of self-worth, but also begin to teach that the ordinary expenses of life are many. In a few years time, the young person will leave foster care. Many will then have to provide for themselves. The current system encourages a dependency culture that may be difficult to lose when the child becomes an adult.

* * *

No one in Maddie's family has ever held a job for more than a few weeks. Her experience of working life was that you went occasionally, when it suited you. There was no regard for employers. After being with us for about a year, through a local youth agency, Maddie was placed at the local SPCA. She loved animals, and her fellow workers took a liking to her.

Two weeks into the job Maddie announced matter-of-factly over dinner, "By the way, I'm not going back any more."

"Oh, why's that?" Andy replied trying to sound neutral.

"Well, it rained today. And it is probably going to rain tomorrow. I'm not going to get wet!" Part of Maddie's task at the SPCA was walking the larger dogs.

As carefully as we could we explained that this is not the way jobs worked.

"Maddie, when you have a job, you go to work every day," Jane said kindly. "That's what Andy and I do. Besides your friends at work will be depending on you now. And what about the dogs? They love it when you pet them, and walk them."

The next day, newly equipped with gloves, boots, and a raincoat Maddie went to work.

We have had a similar conversation many times. A work ethic needs to be habituated, just like most other things in life. It's hard when a child has never had such a work ethic modeled for them.

In Maddie's case, she matured into a lovely young woman. In her subsequent jobs she was described as reliable and responsible. She left us many years ago, but we have watched with interest, and not a little pride, as we have seen her career progress. We have smiled at her Facebook status update, "I don't feel like it, but I suppose I'd better go to work . . ."

We need to acknowledge all the outside help these young people have received to help them on their journey through foster care: Youth Advocacy Program, Job Link, the Advocacy Center (which helps victims of spousal and sexual abuse), the Learning Web, Mental Health Association, the YMCA, and the many employers who through these schemes are willing to employ teens in foster care and mentor them.

Deputies and Cruisers

People who foster teenagers do get to know the police—or, at least, that is our experience. A number of deputy sheriffs and state troopers know us on a first name basis! This is mostly because we have had to file many "missing person" reports for teenage runaways. Foster care can be a little restricting for a teenager. Children in care can't just decide to sleepover at a friend's house. There are procedures: a security check has to be run on all the members of the host family over eighteen. This is a very minimal check, to ensure that no one has committed any offenses against children. In order to do this check, the adults have to sign a form giving permission to DSS. It is quite simple really, if a little time-consuming. Once the check has been carried out, it is left to the discretion of the foster carer when visits can take place. Even so, however minimal the process, we have only ever seen one child's friend's parents willing to do the checks. It means that a spontaneous, "Would you like to stay over tonight?" is out of the question. This does not suit those teens who like to do things on the spur of the moment. They feel it is unfair. To register protest, they simply don't come home from school and tell the friend's parents that all is fine. Our next task is very clear. If the teen has not returned by the time of the last bus, or a prior agreed time to be in the house, then we make phone calls—first to the sheriff's dispatch requesting contact with the on-call caseworker. The caseworker will call us back, and we explain the situation. We usually agree on a time to report news. If the child has not returned by the agreed time, we call the sheriff's dispatch. In due course, we watch the deputy's cruiser turn into the driveway—hopefully without lights flashing! (Though we suspect the neighbors are used to seeing patrol vehicles at our home.) We fill in a report. The deputy leaves. During the night, if the child does not return, we will likely receive more calls from the on-call caseworker and from the deputy before his shift ends. In other words, it is a late night, followed by interrupted sleep and an early morning.

When the child returns safe and sound, he wonders why we are bleary-eyed, and without quite the usual amount of patience. When we explain he has technically been a runaway he feels offended. "I was only at my friend's house!" As one teenager told us, "Teenage years are meant to be fun."

Although we have filed reports on many occasions, we have only had a couple who were truly runaways. All the others we knew were just taking time to be with friends and would turn up the next day. (Though still we have to follow procedures, just in case.) The true runaways are usually older teens who don't want to be in foster care or who know they will soon be going to residential care. Often they have looked after themselves, and other family members, since early childhood. It seems ridiculous to them that they can't be on their own at fifteen or sixteen. Often they are trying to avoid the system. Unfortunately, sometimes friends and birth families have helped to conceal them.

* * *

Jane answered the phone, "Hello Jane, this is Amber."

Jane's response was quick, "Amber we have been so worried, you've been missing ten days."

"I know, I just wanted to let you know that I'm fine," came Amber's response.

"Well, I'm really glad to hear from you," Jane said, "Where are you?"

"If I tell you, will you have to tell the caseworker?" Amber retorted swiftly.

"Yes, I will," Jane said, "I can't keep that to myself."

"Okay, I'm not going to tell you then, but I will phone again," Amber's answer was not unexpected.

Jane and Amber continued to chat generally about her well-being. Later Jane was able to report to the caseworker that she knew Amber was safe but had no idea where she was. Our expectation was that she would try to keep undetected until she reached her eighteenth birthday and could sign herself out of foster care.

*　*　*

Often teenagers come to us with a mental health diagnosis, often accompanied by psychiatric medication. The diagnoses are many and varied: bipolar disorder, attention deficit hyperactivity disorder (ADHD), post traumatic stress disorder (PTSD), obsessive compulsive disorder (OCD), oppositional defiance disorder (ODD), reactive attachment disorder (RAD), and depression are among the most common. Regardless of the diagnosis the truth is we face sad, confused, and angry young people. Suicide threats, cutting, and eating disorders are often the way these things manifest.

According to the organization Young Minds in the United Kingdom:

- 1 in 10 children and young people aged 5–16 years suffer from a diagnosable mental health disorder—that is around three children in every class.
- Between 1 in every 12 and 1 in 15 children and young people deliberately self-harm.
- There has been a big increase in the number of young people being admitted to hospital because of self-harm. Over the last ten years this figure has increased by sixty-eight percent.
- More than half of all adults with mental health problems were diagnosed in childhood. Less than half were treated appropriately at the time.
- Nearly eighty thousand children and young people suffer from severe depression.
- Over eight thousand children aged below ten years suffer from severe depression.
- Seventy-two percent of children in care have behavioral or emotional problems—these are some of the most vulnerable people in our society.
- Ninety-five percent of imprisoned young offenders have a mental health disorder. Many of them are struggling with more than one disorder. (YoungMinds.org.uk)

We have made occasional emergency trips to the hospital for psychiatric evaluations. We have worried over girls who don't want to eat.

We have seen the result of anger that results in smashed Xboxes or things thrown around bedrooms.

* * *

D.T. had broken several of his possessions. The anger inside reared up at trivial things. It was never directed at people; only at things. He had smashed three Xboxes. We had on many occasions talked with him about trying to control the anger, and not letting it control him. We had learnt that when we heard his voice raised from the basement playroom, we should try to head it off by an early intervention. On this occasion we heard a roar.

"D.T. what's up?" asked Andy. D.T. was clearly beyond speech. His fist poised over the Xbox.

"D.T. think! Don't let the anger control you," Andy spoke firmly, "You can do this, you can beat it."

"Go on D.T. We know you can do it," Jane encouraged.

We continued to encourage him for several minutes as his fist remained motionless in the air. Eventually, with a huge physical effort that we could actually see on his face, he safely lowered the fist. A huge grin spread across his face. He had done it and he was so proud of himself. D.T. never smashed anything again. He had learned that he could control anger.

Stealing

An issue that we have faced many times with teens is stealing. If a teenager is using drugs, or drinking alcohol, he needs money to buy these things. Many of our teenagers have had jobs, but when substance abuse is a problem it is unlikely that the teen will be able to hold down a job. Of course, not all stealing is drug related.

* * *

Andy commented, "Jane, have you seen my little Apple battery charger and the rechargeable batteries for the iPad keyboard."

"No! No idea where it is," Jane replied.

"It was plugged in here and it's gone. Are you sure you haven't moved it?" was his response.

"No, definitely not seen it."

Something else had gone missing! We thought we had a thief in the house. We had noticed a number of other things had disappeared. Sadly, many of the teens have never developed a consciousness regarding others and their possessions. They simply take what they want. They rarely admit to it. Over the years, much has gone missing.

Some months after this particular incident, Andy found the rechargeable battery pack. He had forgotten that he had taken it to his office at the university. He was glad that none of the children had taken it. But, this incident raises another issue. When it is known that one or more of the children in the home steal, a cloud of suspicion forms. It leaves everyone in an uncertain place. We doubt children's truthfulness, when we ought not to. The reason is that the home runs on trust. When it becomes obvious that trust has been broken, it is very difficult to regain it.

Stealing is not confined to theft from foster carers. We have experienced teens being arrested for shoplifting at the mall. We have also had children steal from other children in the home, which is always so sad to see. Twice children in our home have had bikes stolen by other foster children. Other things belonging to teens have also gone missing: iPods, chargers, clothing, and bus passes, to mention but a few.

Some of the time victims press legal charges against our teens. If convicted, this usually results in probation with regular visits to a probation officer, or an adjournment in contemplation of dismissal. This means that, if the offender can keep out of trouble for a period specified by the judge, the charges will be dropped.

One of the more sobering facets of stealing is that some of the children were taught to steal when they were young by their parents. A pair of young teenage sisters told us how their dad showed them how to steal cookies from the local store. Other parents have taken their children to steal clothes and electronics. As foster carers we try to impart to foster children some empathy for the victims of their theft, but in many cases they don't "get it."

* * *

It had been a long day for Jane: up at 6:00 AM; out to work by 7:30; a crazy day at school with multiple kids in meltdown. It was always the same as the Holidays drew near. Having made a cup of tea she sat with Samantha who had just arrived home, debriefing on the day. Ronny clattered through the kitchen door and scooted past quickly, hoping Jane did not see his book bag looking twice the size it was when he left for school.

"Ronny, what's in your bag?" she called after him pleasantly.

"Oh, nothing at all," he shouted back as he made his way clumsily up the stairs.

It didn't take long to ascertain that Ronny had stuffed his bag with a Jets football shirt, matching socks, and a pair of used cleats.

Ronny did not have any spare cash. He routinely spent his allowance within an hour or so of receiving it.

"So, how did you pay for these?" Jane asked, concerned as Ronny had a history of stealing—nothing major, odd things from other children in the group home he was placed in before he came to us.

"I've got a receipt for them!" he responded petulantly throwing the piece of paper roughly in Jane's direction.

The receipt was from a local store that traded in used sports equipment. According to the receipt he had received $30.00 for sundry sports items, had spent $25.99, and had been given $4.01 in change. This he had spent on candy at the drug store nearby.

To receive $30.00 credit from the sports store would require items valued considerably more. We knew that he did not have items to trade. Jane took Ronny back to the store the next day. It transpired that Ronny had taken several racquetball racquets and balls and three baseball gloves that belonged to us. One of the racquets was virtually new and had been a gift to Andy from a good friend, who had subsequently died. The raquet had deep sentimental value. By the time Jane visited the shop that racquet had already been sold, as had the better of the baseball gloves. The store manager was full of apologies, but the damage had been done. We estimated that Ronny had taken almost $300 worth of our equipment to get his $30. Subsequently we checked the games cupboard and found Ronny had also traded an Xbox and about a dozen games at a different store. We never did find out how much he received for the several hundred dollars worth of gaming gear, nor what he spent the money on.

Sex

The other big challenge with the foster care of teenagers is dealing with sexual issues. We have always taken boys and girls together as we believe that teenagers need to be able to relate to each other in a normal way. Obviously sometimes we end up with all girls or all boys. Yet, we do have to be wise about whom we take. Once, having taken a teenage girl in good faith, we learned a few days later that she had made accusations of rape against several teenage boys. All the accusations had proved unfounded. However, investigations had been carried out. At the time we had two teenage boys in the house. We asked that the girl be placed elsewhere. It is always sad to do that, but we felt it necessary in order to protect the two who had been with us a while.

We do have a few minor rules around boys and girls. First and foremost, there can be no relationships within the household. We explain that it is just too complex especially when the relationship ends. So far as we know, the teenagers have understood that, and have been respectful of it. Second, no boys are allowed in girls' bedrooms, and vice versa. However, we have had to amend it, as over the last few years we have had three or four teenagers who had same gender orientation. Some of the other children pointed out that the boy/girl rule is no longer fair. We concurred. We now say that no one should be in another's bedroom without our permission. We make our decisions on a case-by-case basis.

Other sexual considerations are usually around safe sex and birth control. We do not want to encourage promiscuous relationships with a different partner each week. Nor do we want teenage pregnancies or sexually transmitted diseases. Therefore, we talk to the children about relationships, which includes keeping themselves safe. We have had children as young as twelve who are consensually sexually active. We long ago realized that the most important issue for us was to keep sexually active children safe. This includes making sure that teenagers of both sexes visit planned parenthood. Knowing that they will have sexual relationships, we think responsible re-parenting is to ensure they do so safely. This is a fine line to walk, and we do not want to encourage a sexualized childhood. Yet, once a youngster has lost innocence and is sexually active, it is mostly too late to change. At this juncture safety from disease, and from pregnancy for girls, becomes the most important factor. This is pragmatic rather than ideal.

We have realized, also, that we need to be diligent to ensure that correct instruction is given. It is a mistake to think that a teen with a history of sexual abuse knows about healthy sexuality or about pregnancy or disease. For some, too, sex is little more than a game without consequences.

According to the Center for Disease Control (CDC), in 2014, 47.4 percent of United States teenagers have had sexual intercourse, 33.7 percent during the previous three months. Nearly half of the nineteen million STDs each year are among the age group 15–24. In 2009, 400,000 girls aged 15–19 years gave birth. However, according to the Child Trends Data Bank (2014), sexual activity among teens is marginally down for White and Hispanic teens, and down from fifty-nine percent to forty-one percent for Black teens from 1991 to 2011.

Substance Abuse

We have frequently taken teens with substance abuse issues—smoking, drugs, and alcohol.

Many of the teenagers we have cared for smoke cigarettes. In New York State, foster carers are not allowed to smoke in rooms that the children will be in. That has not been an issue for us, as neither of us smoke. (Jane was never tempted. Andy tried it in his early teens for a few weeks, but didn't take to it.) However, almost all the teenagers we have had living with us do smoke, and many are addicted. They are underage and, according to the foster care regulations, we cannot allow them to smoke on our property. Nor can we purchase cigarettes for them.

However, we also need to be realistic. Therefore, when a teenager is placed with us as we explain how the household works we always ask them if they smoke. If they say "yes" we explain our rules about it. If they say no, we tell them that we think that is a good decision, but explain the rules regardless! The rules are quite simple. There is to be absolutely no smoking in our house, in the driveway, on the deck, or in the garden. There is absolutely no leaving the driveway and standing smoking outside the neighbors' houses. The smoker has to take a short walk, cross the road, and move a little way up the street to where there are no houses.

We ask that lighters be left downstairs in the kitchen. We learned this after an experience with two teenage boys. Creatively, they invented a game that involved spraying deodorant and setting it on fire. They played this game in their bedrooms! We also stopped buying spray deodorant!

By and large, we have found that teenagers have been respectful about our smoking rules. We have had a couple of instances where someone smokes in the house—usually in winter, when it's cold and snowy outside. Our home is heated by forced air. When someone smokes in one room (often the bathroom) the smell of cigarettes quickly permeates the rest of the house. The bad habit is nipped in the bud.

We have experienced teenagers who just smoke to look "cool." For them, at least at this stage, it is not an addiction. We have also had teenagers who are seriously addicted to cigarettes. Some of them were introduced to cigarettes as young children. After ten years of smoking, the habit is deeply ingrained. Those teens who are addicted to nicotine are very jittery and on edge if they don't have access to a cigarette.

Interestingly, over the years whenever we ask what age they started smoking the answer is often "eight." We are not quite sure why eight, but that is the age frequently given. Perhaps, that is just another way of saying, "As long as I can remember."

* * *

Jane was transporting a group of girls to the mall. The girls' conversation came around to smoking. Jane pricked up her ears.

"So Cheryl why don't you smoke? You scared?" said Ramona, to our foster child.

"Me scared? I could kick your ass any day!" Cheryl fake punched Ramona.

"So what then?"

"Tried it and didn't like it."

"When?"

"I was about eight. My dad made me. Said I needed to grow up. Smoked it and hated it."

"You were just a kid. Try it again."

"No thanks. Loser!"

* * *

We have also taken teenagers who are already dealing with alcoholism or addicted to drugs, many coming to us through the JD/PINS route. Often their families have similar problems. They have known no other way of life. We must say, sadly, that as a group these are the children in whom we see the least changes. Often, these older teenagers in foster care see "the system" as the lesser of two evils. It's a choice between foster care or jail. By late teens they have already developed habits and character traits that are difficult to change.

On more than one occasion we have had teens try to persuade us to let them have wine or beer with a meal. These have been as young as twelve or thirteen. They cannot understand why we say no. In their eyes we are being "mean."

On at least four occasions we have had phone calls from the police asking us to go to the hospital. Young people whom we were fostering had ended up drunk, or under the influence of drugs, to such an extent they had ended up being transported to the hospital with fears for their health and safety.

It is very sobering (forgive the pun!) to see the young people in a terrible state when we arrive at the hospital. They don't recognize us, they are often dribbling, and they are talking incoherently. It is a sad situation. Fortunately none of our teenagers to date have suffered long-term effects. We were able to pick them up the next day and take them home. In most of these cases they went with friends straight after school to drink for several hours.

It raises huge questions about the hereditary nature of alcoholism and addiction. It would be wrong to give the impression that all the children who have problems in this area come from families who do. That is certainly not the case. However, we have seen that correlation on several occasions. When children learn behavior from their parents and caregivers, simply accepting that substance abuse is the norm, we are not surprised at the correlation.

One young woman who lived with us from the age of fourteen had suffered severe harm because of the substance abuse of her parents. She was adamant that she would not go the same way. She was very against drugs and alcohol and, repeatedly, told us she would never drink or take drugs. Sadly, about five years later a friend introduced her to alcohol. From that moment she was hooked. It felt like it was out of her control. Happily, after a couple of extreme experiences, she was able to see that it really was harming her. Many years later, as an adult, she has not succumbed to alcoholism. But, it continues to be a struggle for her.

As foster carers one of the things we have had to do is to try and recognize whether a teenager has a real problem with substance abuse.

According to the National Institute on Drug Abuse (2014), the major drug use by teens is marijuana (36.4 percent). However, use of drugs by teens has declined steadily since 1991, except for the use of heroin, which has risen slightly.

We have also had teenagers who have come to us from rehab. It is often sad to see how institutionalized some children become. Some even ask permission to use the bathroom. It takes a few weeks for them to relax. As with all aspects of fostering, some of these teenagers are a success, some do not do so well. Although the rehab placement has tried to help them it is also an isolating place. The move from rehab to foster care allows a new sense of freedom. This can be very positive, but also there are suddenly all the old temptations to face. Sadly, for some it is too much.

Erica came to us after an eighteen-month stay in rehab. The case-worker who asked us if we could give her a home, explained how well she had done and how successfully she had completed her treatment plan. We welcomed her and for a week or two she did really well. She settled into her new school. Her name was added to our family membership at the YMCA, where she enjoyed sports. All the early signs were good. Then, after only a couple of weeks, she met a friend from her past. We were concerned, but she assured us that all was well. We continued to keep a close eye on her. Our instinct was that things were deteriorating, but all the outward signs still showed her doing everything well. However, we had been fostering for a long time and knew that the outward signs can be faked. We were a little worried. Then one morning Jane went down to the laundry room in the basement. The window was broken, mud and debris were on the floor. Clearly someone had broken in.

Much discussion ensued during which all our current foster children assured us that they knew nothing about it. We were not sure we really believed their stories. As nothing had been taken it had all the hallmarks of an "inside job." Someone had entered the house after all was locked up. However, our policy with the teens is always to make no accusations. The police were called. After they had surveyed the scene, they also talked to the teenagers, wondering if perhaps friends had come to visit! It transpired that Erica had quickly slipped back into the drug scene. Her habit had been to sneak down in the early hours and leave a basement window unlatched. That night in her drugged state she had tried to get in through the wrong window! She had been doing this every night since she had met her friend. With the caseworker, we decided that her behavior was too unsafe for her to remain in foster care. Sadly, she had to return to a residential setting. We heard a couple of years later that as an adult she was in prison, convicted of drug- and violence-related crimes.

Happily, not all teenagers who come from rehab regress in that way. A young man came after a few months in rehab. He seemed timid and constantly worried that he might do wrong. Yet, we could sense a determination and inner strength about him. He wanted to do well. And he did! He completed his studies, graduated from high school, and went on to community college. He has kept in touch and we know that he is doing really well. There were some bumps and relapses along the way, although nothing sufficient to require further treatment. He is now attending university and doing well. We are eager to see what the future holds for him.

On one occasion we had to advocate against sending a teen to rehab. He was already in a local drug program, and had been doing very well. Then there came a time when he tested positive for marijuana. The young man told us that it was a very brief relapse. We believed him. However, the local program felt they could no longer let him continue, and they made a decision that he needed to go to a residential setting. We wanted to see him be given another chance to prove his intention of staying clean. The caseworker supported us giving him another chance. We had several meetings—some very difficult—with the program director and staff.

In the end, the decision was made that he could enter another local program. This meant he could stay with us, rather than going away. We felt it was another example of young people being judged negatively because they were in foster care. We were quite sure if this had been a child from a "normal" middle class family, residential rehab after just one slip would not have happened. This particular young man did very well. From later conversations with him, it had been a new experience to have someone willing to advocate for him.

7

A Question of Ethics:
How Shall We Live?

Values

At this juncture we want to look a little deeper at values and the ethics we derive from them. Everything we have considered so far relates to what is the best life for children. How might we re-parent children whose birth parents cannot care for them? What kind of re-parents are needed to fulfill this task?

Andy is a moral philosopher, a professional ethicist. At parties and in casual interactions, that's a conversation stopper! That is until Andy explains that ethics is issues of right and wrong, what is good and bad, and questions about the way we should live. It seems everyone has an opinion about that! Moral philosophers move beyond mere opinions to do the careful work of trying to find out why we think some things are right and some wrong, and about how we decide what is good and bad. They look at what great thinkers in the past said about this, compare systems of ethical thought, and apply logical reasoning to try to make sense of it all.

At its core, ethics and morality—for the time being let's assume they are the same thing—are about what is important to us and what we value. Why do we value one thing and not something else? Why is kindness valued more highly than spitefulness? Why is telling the truth valued more often than telling lies, but on occasion a well-chosen lie might be better? Why is sex between consenting twenty-somethings okay, but sex between consenting fourteen-year-olds perhaps not so? Most readers will already be finding fault with something we've just written, and working out a better answer! And the answer you are thinking of will be based on your values—those fundamental things about the world that you think are true and important.

Values, then, are important and our values are pretty close to who we are on the inside. The things we value most are what we call "the good." When we come across something that cuts across our values we tend to think of it as "bad." Further, we desire more of the things we value most. "Things" in this context are not just "stuff," or material items you can place a monetary value on. For instance, most people value respect. Because we place a high value on respect, we tend to want more of it and not less. When someone is disrespectful, their disrespect cuts across our value of respect, and we consider that bad. In the contemporary world, we have raised our highest values to the status of rights. In the eighteenth century, when rights were first being talked about, early modern people valued being alive, accompanied by freedom, and the desire to seek a happy life—a life of well-being. Those ideas were immortalized in the words of the United States Declaration of Independence. "All men [sic] are created equal and are endowed by their creator with certain inalienable rights, among which are life, liberty and the pursuit of happiness." Those rights were based on bottom-line values. It was as if the framers of the Declaration said, "These are the most important things we can think of."

It's also true that most of the time our values are in the background of life. They are close to our core, yet we take them for granted. Values usually come to the foreground when something we hold deeply is challenged. Recently, we read an interesting story in an online British newspaper. A businessman, a small contractor who worked from his home, had been robbed a number of times over the previous year. He had lost several thousand pounds of equipment, and suffered much damage. Though the man reported every incident to the police, the police said there was nothing they could do about it. He would just have to take the losses. One evening three youthful burglars broke into his house, thinking the businessman was out of town. He chased them away, wielding a cricket bat (in the United States it would have been a baseball bat). Catching one of the burglars, during a scuffle the business-man hit him several times, breaking the burglar's arm. In the ensuing court case, the businessman was found guilty of causing the robber injury and was sent to jail for a few weeks. He was also ordered to pay compensation to the robber who was injured. There was a public outcry. Some people were angry that the businessman was punished for protecting his property. Some were angry at the criminal justice system that "always lets the vandals get away with it." Some were angry that the man had "taken the law into his own hands." What happened is that values people held dearly were challenged—values such as "fairness," "just deserts," "it's wrong to reward bad behavior," and "only the police may use legitimate violence." These values and others came to the fore, and some of the values conflicted. It became easy to see what was important to people when their latent values were challenged.

Or, think about the checkout line at the supermarket. A child is constantly fingering the candy on the too-low shelf. Eventually she breaks in two a number of candy bars. Her father is next to the girl, sees what she is doing, but ignores her. The older woman in the line behind the child is beginning to fume. You can almost hear her thoughts, "Why doesn't he do something about that? What kind of parent would allow a child to behave like that? Hasn't he taught her any manners? What a badly behaved child!" Though the woman may not have thought about it, when her values about parenting and children's behavior are challenged they come to the fore. Her mental gymnastics are playing with her moral sense, and her moral sense is shaped by what she values the most. In this instance, she values a certain kind of "proper" behavior for children. She values a certain style of parenting. When you value something important, that value shapes the kind of person you want to be, and how you want others to be too. Your values become your ethos—your ethics.

Ethics, Rules, and Punishment

If we hear of ethics in everyday life it is usually in the media and is about an "ethics infringement," or the "Senate Ethics Committee," or some such thing. This popular image of ethics suggests that morality deals with rules for behavior, compliance with the rules, and punishments for infractions. It's an important part of ethics, and is the basis for those aspects of ethics that become codified as laws. Ethical rules in any society function as the boundary of acceptable behavior. However, the boundary is perhaps not the most important part. More significant is the way we live within the bounds.

As we have seen, much ethical thinking in western culture owes a great debt to German philosopher Immanuel Kant. It was Kant who gave to our culture the notion that a moral person is one who carries out her obligations or duties. He called the basic rule a categorical imperative— something that is true all the time, in every situation, for all people. The categorical imperative is, too, an ethical rule that can be "universalized." Kant suggested that telling the truth was an example of the categorical imperative. For Kant it was never acceptable, in any circumstance, to tell a lie. This is a universal ethical rule. We don't (just for now) want to jump to the obvious criticism that sometimes telling a lie might be the better option than telling the truth. For the moment, it's sufficient to understand that for Kant the ethical life is about duties, and when duties are discovered (say the duty to tell the truth) these duties should never be broken.

Kant is a complex and important philosopher and this is to oversimplify his position. However, this is the way Kant has influenced our culture. This oversimplification has permeated much of our thinking about morality in the modern western world. Morality is often about knowing the rules and keeping them. If you don't keep the rules, then there is a consequence, often a punishment, which you must bear. Hence, "ethics committees" in organizations act as institutional enforcers of correct behavior. Such committees spend their time and attention on those who commit "ethics infringements." If you are called before the ethics committee, chances are you have been accused of breaking some rule or other. If you are found guilty, the committee will apply the agreed-on punishment.

This is fine so far as it goes. All societies and all institutions need boundaries that mark the unacceptable from the acceptable. An argument can be made that punishment acts as a deterrent to others who might think twice before they also cross the boundary. This is clear when the boundaries mark interpersonal relationships—including what is acceptable to do to other people's bodies. As a culture, probably since the 1970s, we have become more aware that it is just not acceptable to do things to other people's bodies without their permission. Our awareness has resulted in setting boundaries around such issues as sexual harassment, inappropriate touch, and the like. The boundaries, and the associated rules and consequences for rule-breaking, have shifted.

However, to think merely about the boundaries of the permissible is a limited and poor way of considering the ethical task in its entirety. Ethics, being more than rules, compliance, and punishment for non-compliance, is about what would make for a good and well-lived life. For our purposes in this book, what would a good, well-lived life be for children, and what would it look like for their carers?

Ancient Ethics for Today

An older view of ethics (held by most of the ancient Greek and many Asian philosophers) was that morality was not so much about rule keeping, but more about being a certain kind of person—a person who has certain character traits. The kind of person who has developed these character traits (called virtues in philosophy) is likely to be a person who lives a good life, a life of personal thriving, and someone who has good relationships with others. Also, in simple terms, a virtuous, hence moral, person is more likely to carry out virtuous or moral actions than a person of vicious character. The Greeks knew that even the best rule-book is useless unless people were psychologically equipped to keep the rules. Ethics, as we have noted before, is the way we answer the questions, "How shall we live?" and "What would a good life look like?"

In the ancient world, the Greek philosopher Aristotle and the Chinese philosopher Confucius exemplified this broader conception of ethics (though shared by many others). Their philosophies have become once again fashionable, among philosophers, since the early 1980s and have been coined "virtue ethics." Virtue ethics asks not "What are the rules I need to follow to be ethical?" but rather "What kind of person do I need to be to live a good life?" Though not opposed to either rules or techniques, virtue ethics suggests that all the rules and techniques in the world will be useless unless the person who seeks to keep the rules and use the techniques *is a certain kind of person.* Then when you are a virtuous person, you probably don't need the rules.

This way of looking at ethics is far reaching. For the purposes of this book, it has implications for what it means to be a re-parent, and what it means to carry out the re-parenting task. For foster carers and adopters, the emphasis will not be on rules and techniques, but on how to become a certain kind of person who will best be able to re-parent children. Rather than just teaching children to keep the rules, re-parenting is about helping children become certain kinds of people.

This way of thinking about ethics has become known as Neo-Aristotelianism and was brought to light most recently by philosopher Alasdair MacIntyre (see MacIntyre 1985, 1988, 1990, 1999). Before Macintyre began his work, Aristotle was somewhat out of fashion. MacIntyre gave the Aristotelian tradition of virtue ethics a new lease of life. Like virtue ethicists before him, MacIntyre looked at how people might become virtuous, that is, how they might best develop the type of character to enable them to live well, for to live well is to know happiness.

Learning from MacIntyre, and simplifying him somewhat, we suggest that we become virtuous in a fourfold process:

1. Discover that which we value most.
2. Find the goal (*telos* in Greek) that these values suggest.

3. Develop the virtues (traits of character) that enable us to fulfill that *telos*.
4. Build the habits that develop the virtues.

Philosophers have discussed at length how a *telos* is chosen or discovered, and whether a *telos* is "built in." Aristotle, for instance, believed that everything has a natural *telos*. The *telos* of an acorn is to become an oak tree. Aristotle assumed that human beings, too, have a natural *telos*. He thought it was happiness, or well-being. However, not all philosophers are convinced that there is a natural human *telos*, but that debate need not detain us. There is less debate that a *telos* may be chosen (what Andy has termed "elective teleology" 2012, 32, 91). Returning to Aristotle, if we choose the goal of well-being, or happiness, then we will pursue those aspects of life that lead to happiness. It is those aspects of life that we value. So, for a happy life (if that is the chosen goal), values such as freedom from pain, a sense of purpose and accomplishment, enough money to live comfortably, being able to participate in decisions that affect us, and good relationships with other people, would all be important. The chosen goal contains underlying and hidden values.

Then further, for Aristotle that which leads to the goal of happiness is a certain way of being human—that is, people with certain character traits are most likely to reach the goal. When the goal and its values are clear, then the kind of person who can achieve that goal also becomes clear. She will be the kind of person with certain virtues. The final piece of the Aristotelian puzzle is how do you get those virtues or character traits? The answer is by building habits. For example, for Aristotle, a well-lived life is one where courage is valued. For someone to reach that goal, they would need to become a courageous person (that is, have the virtue of courage). You become a courageous person by daily building the habit of doing courageous things. As you do the daily habit of courageous acts (even little ones) then in time those habits "solidify" into a courageous character.

Aristotle did not say much about kindness. However, let's say that to live a good life, kindness is something we value. To become a kind person (to have the virtue of kindness) then becomes important. How do you become a kind person? By carrying out on a daily basis the habit of kindness. Occasional acts of kindness might not make you a kind person. But, building habits of kindness, even small acts of kindness, over time become a virtue, a character trait. Many and repeated acts of kindness make you a kind person.

If you are new to this way of thinking about ethics it can seem a little complicated. If you have stayed with us so far, congratulations! You are doing philosophy! If we simplify this Neo-Aristotelian way of looking at things, we can ask four questions:

1. What do I value most?
2. What goal do those values suggest I make my own?
3. What kind of person do I need to be to accomplish that goal with those values?
4. How do I become that kind of person?

You could apply this kind of thinking quite expansively and do this exercise for your life as a whole. However, in this book we want to do the exercise with those who care for children in foster care and those who have become adoptive parents. Remembering that the children we care for have been victims of violence in varying ways—through maltreatment, neglect, and perhaps abuse—what values do we bring to the task? What should we be aiming at? What is the goal?

For those who become carers, it's likely that underlying values will include loving kindness, care, fairness, freedom from harm, a good chance at life, and such like. When we apply those values we quickly realize what needs children in care have. Their needs become our chosen goal. We can summarize these values and associated needs to say that children in care need to be well re-parented, need to be loved, and need to be free from violence and harm. In short, the goal we have chosen for our life as foster carers is "Loving Nonviolent Re-parenting."

As a re-parent, having chosen the goal what kind of person do I need to be to reach the goal? What character traits are required? And just how do I become this type of person? What habits of life need to be developed? We will consider this below.

Making Nonviolence the Goal

It is illegal in New York State for foster carers to use physical punishment. Though foster carers must agree in their training that no form of physical violence will be used, from our experience, not all foster carers and adopters have internalized the values of nonviolence. During the training for potential foster carers, a whole session is spent on helping attendees understand why physical punishment is counterproductive in caring for children. At the end of the session, facilitators speak about the law regarding corporal punishment of children in foster care. After the session one attendee asked, "Will I be able to spank him when needed when he is adopted?" The person asking the question was a gentle, kind man. Yet he saw spanking as a valid and helpful form of discipline. Clearly, the state law was seen merely as one more layer of bureaucracy to pay lip service to. The idea of nonviolence had not been internalized as a good in itself. Underlying this is a deep-seated belief that children are "ours," in much the same way that property is "ours." We do with that which is "ours" things which we would not consider doing with the property of others. While children "belong to" the state, the rules say that corporal punishment is not allowed. When the child "becomes mine," the rule no longer applies.

Part of our current work is to try to help foster carers internalize nonviolence for its own sake not because it is the law. The need is clear. A loving nonviolent home, where children are welcomed, is part of a larger understanding of nonviolence as a way of living. Perhaps coincidentally, we have been nonviolentists for almost as long as we have been foster carers. We trace our nonviolentism to the early 1980s, though our stories differ.

In the summer of 1983 Andy attended the Royal Army Chaplain's Department recruitment conference at Bagshot Park in Surrey. At the time he was a trainee Baptist minister studying for ordination at the Northern Baptist College, Manchester, UK. Trainee ministers were required to do several weeks each year working with some form of chaplaincy, in part to see the variety of work ministers are required to do; in part, to see if there was a particular branch of chaplaincy work that seemed appealing. With another colleague, he had chosen to look into military chaplaincy. In 1982, the United Kingdom went to war with Argentina over the disputed Falkland/Malvinas Islands in the South Atlantic. The short, bellicose, and bloody conflict cost the lives of 649 Argentinians and 255 British. It is significant events such as this that cause people to question long-held, and often untested, views. Growing up in England we had simply assumed that what England did was right. The early socialization of children in terms of nationalism and patriotism had worked on us in much the same way it works the world over. My country—right or wrong.

At that time, Andy had already had a long interest in the British military, coming from a long line of warriors, the Falklands Conflict held a morbid fascination for him, as he, and most of the British people, sat glued to the television watching the daily reports of battles and casualties. As a civic-minded young man he seriously considered in what way he might serve Queen and Country. Certain of his call, at that time, to Christian ministry an obvious avenue to explore was military chaplaincy.

And so it was that Andy was enjoying a pre-dinner drink in the Officers' Mess at the home and training center of the army chaplain's department. Glass of beer in hand, he was pondering the ornate depiction of the chaplain's cap badge above the fireplace. Its motto, one of only two British Army regiments written in English rather than Latin, read "In This Sign Conquer," at the center of a stylized cross, with a crown above it. From reading history, Andy knew that this phrase was part of the supposed vision that the Roman Emperor Constantine had seen in the clouds on October 28, 312 CE. Following a further dream in which he met Christ, the Emperor realized that it was by using the sign of the cross that he would defeat his enemies. Whatever the truth behind the legend, the events marked a major change in the relationship of Christianity to the state and to the state's frequent use of violence. Christian crusaders later used stylized crosses as weapons to kill Muslims and Jews in the Holy Land. Such "Christian violence" seemed antithetical to the life of Jesus of Nazareth who taught people to turn the other cheek, refrain from violence, and love enemies.

As Andy pondered his surroundings at Bagshot Park and the unequivocal reference to Constantine, he came to the realization that he was, in fact, a pacifist and that he could go no further with his inquiry into military chaplaincy. In one respect, the decision was very easy. The realization came to him with all the force of a revelation—an unveiling of truth that gripped him and from which there was no escape. He did not seek it. It came as a surprising gift. Yet, in another respect, this realization was also personally difficult. Andy had a nagging feeling that he still wanted to be part of something larger than himself, some great enterprise, and the military certainly offered that. It felt odd to make a decision, not merely to refrain from service, but to turn his back on what he had always considered was a noble and respected profession. While Andy had become instantly clear of his pacifism, he inwardly struggled with the decision for a long time. A colleague, who also attended Bagshot Park, did become a military chaplain and served with honor in the Persian Gulf War. There were times when Andy envied him.

Jane's story is a little different. Like many women she approached life differently from many men—life was more about caring, reciprocation, receptivity than about duty, and contract, and fixed principles. Sara Ruddick, as we have seen, talks about this as "maternal work." For Jane, it was simply the case that violence did not solve issues in any lasting sense, though in 1983 she had not verbalized this as nonviolence. As

Andy began to question the violence of the state and together we read, thought, and talked about war, we came to the conclusion that we were pacifists—that it was never morally right to go to war. For Jane, this gave expression to what she had always intuitively felt.

Over time, we have not changed that viewpoint. Rather, it has been strengthened and we now consider ourselves "nonviolentists"—it is never morally right to use violence to solve conflicts, in personal, family, national, or international life. Nonviolence, in the way we understand and use the term, has both negative and positive elements.

Negatively, nonviolence means to refrain from violent actions. Violent actions include physical violence that causes harm or injury (physical or psychological). But violence, as we have seen, can also be other than physical, when someone uses emotional or psychological means to cause harm. Social systems, too, can be violent. A nonviolentist is someone who seeks to reduce violence in the world in any of those forms. To be nonviolent means to use nonviolence to work against systems of violence.

Positively, nonviolence is very closely associated with loving community. Nonviolence is not simply refraining from violent actions, but to do the opposite—that is to help create loving, caring communities. This is what Martin Luther King Jr. referred to as "Beloved Community."

Accidental Nonviolence

One semester, shortly after finals, Andy was grading a paper for a class he was teaching—*War and Terrorism*. The class can get quite intense, and students have to deal with the darker side of human life. In the nature of the course, some students, having been given glimpses of the worst side of humanity forget the better side. One student began a paper, "For every act of kindness people do, there are thousands of atrocities . . . " Andy had to do some work with the student to help him think this through! In truth, for every atrocity there are thousands of kind and loving actions. For most of us, most of the time, during most of our lives the primary modality of human interaction is one of respect, kindness, compassion. Like Andy's student who had "overdosed" on the course material on war and terrorism, when caring for children who have been neglected, maltreated, and abused, it is sometimes difficult to remember that for most children life is not like that.

Despite living nonviolent lives most of the time, many of us don't really think about nonviolence. We simply don't do violent actions, most of the time. When we do commit acts of violence we most often regret it after the fact. Most people, much of the time, are nonviolentists—but accidentally so. Without thought, attention, or intention we are socialized toward a modality of nonviolence. That is why, when we come across real violence (not the false violence of TV and video games) we are often shocked.

A young woman went into one of our local bars with her girlfriend for a quiet drink. A male approached the girlfriend and punched her in the face, accompanied by a string of verbal abuse for being a lesbian. The man immediately walked out. People in the fairly full bar were simply stunned. By the time those present recovered from the shock of the unexpected violence, the man had disappeared. It was a terrible and violent display of homophobia. The reason for the initial stunned silence was because violence of that kind was not the everyday experience of the clientele of the bar. Most people are nonviolentists in their everyday life without conscious thought about it.

New foster carers are often more stunned than the folk in the bar when they come face to face with the violence their foster children have suffered. Shock is often accompanied by disbelief that adults can be so cruel to children. Their "accidental nonviolentism" is brought to the surface and foster carers have to wrestle with their understanding of violence and nonviolence. What kind of re-parents are they going to be? It is at this point that accidental nonviolence has the potential to transform into intentional nonviolence.

Intentional Nonviolence

If we are correct that at least some (and quite possibly many) foster carers and adopters have not intentionally chosen nonviolence, then our challenge is to help foster carers and adopters internalize the goal of becoming loving nonviolent people. In large measure, this is an educational challenge to expose foster carers and adopters to nonviolent perspectives, understandings, and practice. To this end books and pamphlets explaining the philosophy of love and nonviolence in everyday language are essential; as, too, are courses designed to help foster carers and adopters work through issues of care and nonviolence.

To help think through how we make choices about our goals, we have developed a chart to demonstrate the interconnection of feeling (affective), thinking (reflective) and choosing (elective). The chart is developed from some work Andy has done in writing about how we form moral commitments. These commitments arise in a process that involves conscientization, internalization, and intentionalization.

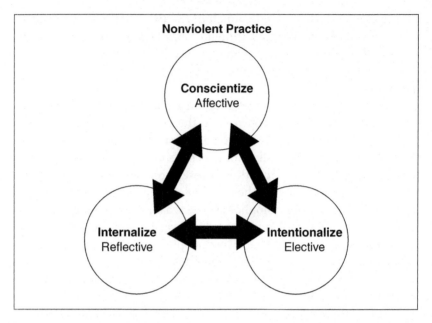

Conscientization (consciousness raising) is that part of the process when we become aware of an issue that we may not have noticed before. As an example, take the human abuse of nonhuman animals. In chapter ten we talk about our commitment to vegetarianism, and for us it is an intimate connection with nonviolence. How did we make that choice? In the first instance we became aware of something that we had completely missed—the way human beings often have little regard for nonhuman animals. We heard about, and later researched, the way animals were used in the meat industry. What we discovered (as many had before us and since) was shocking. Sentient beings that feel pleasure and pain are routinely abused, used merely as "product" facing the cruelest of suffering. The more we read, the more our consciousness about the plight of animals was raised. We were deeply troubled. Our feelings of revulsion, shame, guilt, empathy, sadness, and sense of injustice are all part of what philosophers call "affect." In making choices this affective part of our psyche (our feelings) is often the first element to be stirred.

This same part of the process is essential in becoming a loving non-violent re-parent. It is the stirring of feeling, the affect we experience when we are first conscientized to the plight of children and the effect that violence has had in their lives.

The second part of the process is the internalization of the values of loving nonviolence as we reflect on what violence is, how it affects people, its value in social relationships and communication. To have feelings stirred is good, but is not sufficient in itself to move someone to choose intentionally a nonviolent way of life. Feelings need to be thought about. Why do we feel the way we do? What lies behind those feelings? What values are being challenged? What values are being strengthened? How are we to think about what we feel? In other words, the affective part of the process requires the reflective. In the history of philosophy in the west, the passions (affect, feelings) have always required reason, for control and direction. Though the tradition has often down-played the emotions in favor of the reasoning faculties (and hence the masculine at the expense of the feminine) the tradition at its best highlights the interplay of the two. We need both feeling and thinking for a balanced moral commitment. Feeling without thinking is inexact. Thinking without feeling is cold.

In terms of becoming lovingly nonviolent as a way of life, when we are deeply affected by what we see and understand about children and the violence they suffer, and when we think deeply and carefully about what that all means, we are well on the way to moral commitment.

Yet, feeling about and thinking about are still insufficient. The affective and reflective are only completed in the elective, the choosing of particular courses of action. In other words, when feelings are stirred, and thoughts lend clarity to why we feel a certain way, giving an underlying understanding of the situation, we need to move to action. A loving nonviolent re-parent does not merely empathize with children, or think about the abuse they have suffered and how to repair the damage, he makes a choice to act in a certain way. He refuses to use violence in childcare (physical or emotional). He consciously learns ways of nonviolent communication and conflict solving. He helps the children in his care overcome the effects of violence in their lives. He helps train the children in nonviolence.

Though we have suggested that the process moves from affective, to reflective, to elective, because these three are so interconnected in reality the three happen concurrently. We only analyze to bring clarity to the process. It is through this process that we become intentional rather than accidental nonviolentists.

8

The Long Term: Permanence, Adoption, Returning Home, and Keeping in Touch

Adoption

We do not provide a long-term home for the children we foster, although several have lived with us for a number of years. When we first started to foster we knew that we did not want to adopt and increase our family permanently. Our motivation was that we wanted to help children over a crisis situation, and then help them move on, hopefully having received an amount of healing from their trauma.

When the children leave us it is either to go for adoption, to return to their birth home, or to go into an independent living situation.

Over the thirty plus years we have been fostering, and with the experience of two different countries, we have seen many changes in policy. For babies, who are unable to return home, adoption has always been the goal. That is rarely challenged. However, there have been different opinions over the desirability of long-term fostering over adoption for older children. We know that policies and practices change from state to state and region to region. We can only speak to what we have experienced.

When we were fostering in the United Kingdom the practice was to have two different training routes. One was for people who, like ourselves, wanted to foster. The other was for people who wanted to build a family, or extend their family, through adoption. All the children went to foster care and later, if the courts had terminated parental rights, were matched with an adoptive family. This process sometimes took years. Once an adoptive home was found, the transition from foster care was planned and often took place over several weeks. The time and frequency of visits were dependent on the age of the child and the length of time they had lived with us. We were involved in helping children transition many times. Although it can be sad to see a child go, it is often a joyous occasion.

* * *

One Saturday morning we were woken just before 7:00 AM by the insistent ring of the telephone.

Jane answered, wondering who it was so early on a weekend.

"Hello, is that Jane?" came the unfamiliar voice over the phone.

"Yes, can I help you?" Jane said, still a little puzzled and half asleep.

"The caseworker said I could phone you. He came around last night to tell us about little Julie. We are so excited that we have been offered a child to adopt. We haven't slept at all. I hope this isn't too early. We have been waiting to phone you. We are both here. Can you tell us all about her."

The following conversation lasted about an hour. The couple on the other end of the line could barely contain their excitement as they asked question after question about Julie. They concluded by saying, "We have waited ten years for a child. This is our dream come true."

A few days later this couple got to meet Julie, a healthy toddler who had lived with us for over eighteen months. After that first initial meeting, together with the caseworker, a transition plan was drawn up. Because of Julie's young age and the length of time she had been with us it was decided that the transition should take a month and involve daily contact. We started with visits in our home for a couple of days so they could get to know Julie in familiar settings. This was followed by visits in our home, but we left the premises. Next we visited their home, where we stayed with Julie. This was soon followed by visits alone at the new adoptive parents' home. These increased in duration daily. By the time Julie left us she was going from morning until bedtime. The adoptive parents had become the primary carers. We were pleased to see the attachments growing in this new family unit. Parents and child were bonding together. This was a planned transition that resulted in a successful adoption. The family still keeps in touch with us and sends photos every now and then. Julie has become a fine young woman.

The situation when we came to the United States was slightly different. Prospective adopters and foster carers trained together. In many cases the foster carers were the ones who decided to adopt the children. If the foster carers did not want to adopt, the children were transitioned to preadoptive homes.

On November 19, 1997, President Bill Clinton signed into law the Adoption and Safe Families Act. The stated purpose was "To promote the adoption of children in foster care." The background was the almost constant media attention to "children languishing in foster care." Too many children were spending most of their childhood in multiple homes, never really settling down or finding roots. The Act is quite long. However, the key point is that if children have spent fifteen of the previous twenty-two months in foster care the state has to initiate court proceedings to terminate parental rights. If the parents are working well toward a return home the judge can extend this period of time. In reality, it is often clear before fifteen months whether a child is likely to return home. The Act also allows for children to be freed for adoption sooner in extreme circumstances (See USDHHS 1997).

Undoubtedly, the aims of the Act have been realized in that children can no longer slip through the cracks and move from home to home. The courts have a far greater part to play in the lives of children in care. However, the implementation of the Act has some down sides, at least in our limited experience. The birth parents, especially the mother, now have less power. If a woman has drug or alcohol addiction, fifteen months is often too short a time to turn her life around. In many cases, it is likely that birth children will want to keep some contact with birth parents. Termination of parental rights is often drastic and tragic. In some cases adoption is not the solution, especially for older children. It is very different if the child has been in foster home from birth.

We have argued the case with DSS for the reinstitution of long-term foster care as a valid way of providing children with the safety, stability, and loving care that they need before they move on to independent living. Our suspicion is that many children would thrive given this option. We have cared for teenagers who, for sundry reasons, could not live with their birth parents, but who expressed a wish that, when they become adults, to return home, or at least to have a mature and adult connection with their parents.

* * *

Stevie came to us at fourteen. He loved his mother, but recognized that she could not care for him adequately. Stevie later left us to live on his own, but kept in touch. He was doing well and graduated from college. His birth mother came from another city to cheer him on. A few days later we met Stevie and his mother, quite by chance at the local shopping mall. We chatted for a while, foster carers and birth mother sharing delight in how well Stevie had done. Later that day Stevie posted on Facebook saying how wonderful it was for him to see his birth mother and foster carers together.

* * *

Presently, pressure is on caseworkers to find an adoptive home for these children, as the only "permanent" option. We wonder how many of these children, even having been adopted, will find a way back to their birth families when they are able. We can only imagine the heartbreak for adoptive parents when this happens. For a number of years many of the children we cared for were considered "long term." That is, the likelihood was that the children would be in foster care without adoption for many years, often ending only when the child aged out of the system. With the new laws this type of foster care is no longer possible.

With successful adoptions, we have found that the transition process is a key element in the new relationship. We know from talking with the prospective adopters slow transition can seem an endless process. Often they have waited many years for a child and they just want to take the child home and build a new life. Unfortunately, it is not that simple. At the very least all of the children have suffered the trauma of being taken from their birth families. For many children, foster care is their first experience of stability and routine and now they are being moved again. Those in the process of adoption need to be mindful of this.

Unfortunately, even with care taken many adoptions do break down. We have taken several children and teenagers who have been in pre-adoptive homes or even adopted only to have it break down.

The data from different studies do not show a clear picture (see Child Welfare Information Gateway 2012b). Data are more readily available on disruptions—that is, the ending of adoption procedures after the process has started but before legal adoption. This is because these children remain in the system. Studies show that between nine and twenty-four percent of potential adoptions are disrupted. Data on adoption breakdown is more difficult. Records are often closed after an adoption takes place. Data that is available usually relate to adoptions that break down before a child is eighteen years old and comes back into the public foster care and adoption system. There is no data for private foster care and adoption. Studies found between three and eight percent of adoptions dissolve, with the child returning to foster care. We found no data to show how many teenagers leave their adopted homes in a breakdown after the age of eighteen, or even before with parental consent. However, the various studies show that the older the child on placement, the higher the chance of a disruption or break down.

If adoption is "for life," when the adopted child takes on the same rights and responsibilities as birth children, we would be interested to see how many adoptions do stand the test of time. We would be interested, too, to see how many children who have been adopted seek out their birth parents.

Our first experience of an adoption breakdown was with Alfonso, a seventeen-year-old who stayed with us briefly before going to an independent living program. His story was that he had been adopted as a ten-year-old. Over the ensuing years the early abuse and lack of attachments had caused the relationship with his adoptive parents to become strained. Eventually Alfonso tried to commit suicide. He came to us from a psychiatric hospital still bearing the red scars of his failed attempt. The history of trauma for this young man had simply been too much to overcome. Unfortunately, this is not an isolated incident. We have fostered many teenagers where preadoptive or adoptive placements have disrupted. It is always sad. Both children and preadoptive parents need support to heal. In all cases, counselors and caseworkers work hard to try and resolve the situation. Rarely is it possible to resolve once it has reached the stage where the child has left the home.

We have met many people who have adopted or are waiting to adopt a child. Some of these were at the beginning of the process, adopting a child whom we have fostered. Others are struggling to understand why the placement disrupted. Almost without exception these are kind and caring people who are opening their homes to a child in need. We cannot speak too highly of them. They do amazing work with the children they take. Often taking several children in a sibling group sometimes as large as five or six children. We have known adopters who are couples and singles, straight and gay.

When disruptions happen it is often no one's fault. It is simply a damaged child unable to form the attachments needed to be successful in a family setting. It causes heartbreak for all concerned. When the teenagers "blow out" of a home they can leave a trail of destruction. We have known teens who have stolen from their adoptive parents, sworn at them, and raised fists to hit them, and sometimes used actual violence.

* * *

Ronny, who we met earlier, was a tragic case among many. He came to us twice after preadoption breakdowns. Rejected early in life by an alcoholic mother, abused by her numerous boyfriends, Ronny found it impossible to settle into family life. He was too deeply damaged. His first preadoptive placement was with a mature gay couple. The couple were successful businessmen and had the wherewithal to provide for Ronny's every need. They showered him with love and gifts. Ronny couldn't take it. He returned their love with abuse and violence. After a couple of years the couple could no longer cope with Ronny's lying, stealing, and violence. He was sent from them to a group home where he stayed for a year. To help him "step down" from institutionalization he came to us and spent a more or less trouble-free three months. Another preadoption home was found for him—a late middle-aged husband and wife whose own children had grown and left the nest. This kind couple wanted to give back to society and had decided to adopt. Ronny lasted nine months before he was found stealing from children at school. The stealing was the last straw on top of Ronny's other behavior issues. The couple struggled with a deep sense of failure. Ronny spent another year in detention and came back to us. After another nine months with us Ronny went to his third preadoptive placement. We last heard that this too had broken down. He did not come back to us.

* * *

Before the Clinton legislation, it is likely that Ronny would have been one of the children who drifted through multiple foster homes and detention facilities. Part of the tragedy of his life, was that each pre-adoptive placement gave Ronny the hope of a permanent placement who would be his "forever family." His hopes lifted high by successive caseworkers were dashed. Before he moved to his third preadoption we had wondered if a third breakdown would be one two many. We fear this was the case.

Our hope is that the authorities, case managers, and policy makers will again come to realize the value of providing long-term, loving nonviolent safe homes with trained and experienced loving nonviolent re-parents. This is especially needed for those older children who are so deeply damaged by violence that their adoption is likely to end in heartbreak.

Of course, as the data show, not all adoptions end in disruption, with around eighty percent successful. We know many families who adopted who have wonderful, healthy kids with strong relationships to their parents that will last a lifetime.

Returning Home

Sometimes the children are able to return home. Often this is a result of a lot of hard work on the birth parent's part. They may have been required to do court order substance abuse treatment and parenting classes. The children have visits with them, initially always supervised. Phone calls are encouraged, often put on speakerphone, to ensure that nothing upsetting to the children is said. False promises of return dates are not helpful. As foster carers we found that the amount of phone calls and visits the parent makes is indicative of whether the child will return home or not.

We had only been fostering about three years when we took four-year-old Heidi and her baby half-sister Joni. Heidi's big dark brown eyes, which seemed old in her face, darted everywhere as she took in their new surroundings. As with many children, after their much needed baths and new clothes, the children settled well. A visit to our home by their mom was arranged in a timely fashion. Apparently, she was eager to see her kids. Vouchers were provided for public transport and we agreed to meet the mother at the train station. We were assured by the caseworker that this mother was devastated about losing the children and would definitely not be late. Jane took Heidi with her to meet her mother off the train. Heidi was excited, jumping up and down at the thought that mummy would soon be here. Together, they watched as the train came up the track and the doors opened. The birth mother did not get off the train. Quickly excitement turned to tears as the realization that the visit was not going to happen dawned on Heidi. Subsequent visits were arranged, but mom never turned up.

We learnt from this experience and never again took a child to meet a parent off public transport. We treated future visits very low key, "your mom may be visiting today." We continue this today, never promising a child that a visit will happen. Our language is full of "might" or "possibly," or "sometimes," especially for young children, we simply avoid mentioning the plan, letting the visit be a surprise. Caseworkers are often helpful in trying to minimize disappointment of birth parents not turning up. They often put safeguards into place, for example, requiring the parent to confirm the afternoon before the visit. If the confirmation is not received then the visit is canceled so the child is not left waiting for the parent.

Heidi and Joni stayed with us for about a year. Ultimately their parents' rights were terminated. They were adopted, unusually, into two different families. Separation of siblings is avoided if at all possible. However, if it is proved to be in the best interest of the children a separation of siblings can be obtained. On this occasion, after the long and involved process, it was possible to separate the siblings. In this case, the abuse history was so severe that it was felt they would thrive separately. The court often orders contact between the children, and the adoptive families have to be prepared to facilitate this. In this case the contact was not just between our two as there were several older siblings involved as well. We had hosted all the children on several occasions, as had the other foster carers involved.

We were involved in transitioning Heidi and Joni to their new homes. Again it was a slow and well-planned process. Our policy with younger children who are adopted is to tell the adoptive parents that we are available to help them if needed. We will not contact them, but leave the decision to them about whether they want to keep in touch. Some do, others don't, and either of the decisions is fine with us. We love to hear how the children are, but we are also very aware that this is a new family unit who may not want a foster carer in the background. After the initial transition both of these two new families let us know how Heidi and Joni were doing, but then we did not hear from them again. Several years later we bumped into Joni's adoptive father in a busy shopping center. He greeted us warmly, then pulled photographs out of his wallet showing Joni as a lovely ten-year-old. He was very much the proud father and we were delighted that the adoption had been successful.

On more than one occasion a noncustodial parent (on occasion even a step-parent) has come forward wanting the children. One parent told us that he had only discovered he had a daughter when she was ten years old. He and the child's mother had split up before the pregnancy was known and she had chosen not to tell him. Often, these noncustodial parents live quite a distance away.

Yet slow transitions are still in the best interest as parent and child reconnect. Occasional weekend visits, lots of phone calls, and often a week or two stay during school vacations help with this process. The commitment and strength of these noncustodial parents has always been a source of healing to their children. One parent amazed us as she drove over a thousand miles each way three times during the transition period.

Independent Living

In New York, when teenagers reach eighteen they can sign themselves out of foster care. We have had some who have done this on their eighteenth birthday. Typically these children came into care as older teens and have always planned to leave the moment they could. Our preference is that they stay longer and that their move is a little more mindful. These teenagers have returned home, gone to other relatives or, as is often the case, moved in with boyfriends or girlfriends. There has been a recent change to the law that allows these young people to re-enter foster care if their move doesn't work out. This is definitely a change for the better.

* * *

"Hello, is that Jane?"

"It is," Jane responded, recognizing the voice and asking, "Is that Alyssa?" How are you doing?"

Jane knew from the local newspaper and other sources that things had not gone well for Alyssa after she had left us. The drug addiction, which she seemed to have under control, had proved too strong. Alyssa had returned to her old ways, and petty crime had followed. She had spent a few short spells in the local jail.

"I messed up!" she said quietly. "Can I come back to you guys?"

Jane explained that we would be willing, but she needed to talk to her caseworker. Jane also said that Alyssa would not be allowed to bring drugs or weapons into the home.

Alyssa seemed happy and said she would contact the caseworker.

Sadly, before anything could be arranged, Alyssa was yet again in trouble and found herself in jail.

A few months later Alyssa called again. The conversation was almost identical. The outcome was much the same too. Alyssa never did return to us. We saw her around town a couple of times and she was always pleased to see us. Her problems escalated and the last we heard she was in jail again for drug- and violence-related incidents.

* * *

It is always in the best interests of teenagers as they mature to leave foster care in a planned way. This move to independent living can be achieved in a number of different ways. The majority of older teens we have fostered have transitioned through a supervised independent living plan. The teens live either alone or sharing with one other person in an apartment within a complex with other teenagers in the program. The accommodation is free (for the teen), an allowance is provided for food, clothing, and daily needs. Help is given to buy food, plan menus, find jobs, attend medical appointments, and ultimately find their own apartment. Room inspections for cleanliness are on a daily or weekly basis. Perhaps the downside is that the teens do often have to transfer to a different school. The teenagers can enter the program while only seventeen, and in exceptional circumstances at sixteen. The move is planned and will often take place to fit in with the young person's educational plans.

Janine, a seventeen-year-old girl, moved in the summer, even though she didn't turn eighteen until the next January. She was mature, had experienced looking after herself for many years, and it was decided that she should start her new school in September rather than move mid-year. This kind of independent living is ideal for teenagers who start to find foster care too restrictive.

Other teenagers leave foster care to go into their own apartments that they find locally. These have always been teenagers who are over eighteen, have finished high school—some even two years of college— and are ready to move to be on their own. They tend to do very well. Still others have left us to go to a residential college out of the area. They tend to return for their first couple of vacations, but seem to outgrow quickly foster care as new experiences are presented to them and new friends made.

We have preferred not to have foster children reach twenty-one. The twenty-first birthday can seem like an impending deadline when the young adult is "thrown out." It is much better to work toward independent living with the foster child taking some responsibility for her future.

Keeping in Touch

"Hey it's been a while! Hope u and Andy are cool. I'll be in the area at the weekend. U be around if I stop by?" read the Facebook private message.

Dawson had been with us for a year some years before. We had seen him succeed at college after a rocky start, and had watched his progress over the years. We had noticed he had just completed his Masters Degree in environmental studies and we joined with the hundred other well-wishers on Facebook.

We arranged lunch, and were thrilled to hear of the new job he would soon be starting out of state. His steady partner would be moving with him, and there is talk of marriage.

* * *

It is often very difficult for teens who sign themselves out of care at age eighteen. Most of them in time overcome huge obstacles to create a decent life for themselves. Some of the girls we cared for became pregnant within a few months of leaving care. We are still in touch with several who had children very young. By and large, they are doing well and raising their children successfully, though some, unable to care adequately, lost their babies fairly soon to the system. Often money is an issue, but we see their children clothed, fed, and loved.

9

Spanking, Discipline, and Nonviolence

The children who were whipped and burned in the past were no naughtier than the children of today, and they ended up no better behaved as adults. On the contrary . . . the rate of impulsive violence of yesterday's adults was far higher than today's. What led the parents of our era to the discovery that they could socialize their children with a fraction of the brute force that was used by our ancestors?
—Stephen Pinker, *The Better Angels of Our Nature*

In 1992, while still living in the United Kingdom, we had the privilege of spending four months in the United States. Andy was on sabbatical and we had been invited to various places for him to minister. We were somewhere on an Interstate in North Carolina, enjoying our first real American road trip.

"Dad, can we listen to some music?"

"Hold on a sec. This sounds interesting."

"Do you know what the proudest moment of my life was . . . " the radio preacher drawled. As visitors from Britain, American voices on real American radio were still a novelty to us. Religious stations were completely outside our experience. (This was the early 1990s. Religious programming came soon afterward to the United Kingdom.)

"My proudest moment was when my little girl had been bad. And her mother said to her 'Honey, when your papa comes home he's gonna switch you good.'"

Jane looked over at Andy. Was this for real? Had we tuned into a radio spoof show?

"Dad, this is really boring, can we listen to some music?"

"In just a minute."

"When I came home from visitation that evening," the preacher continued, "my little girl, she met me at the door, and you know what she was carryin'? She was carryin' the switch. And she looked up into my eyes, and she says, 'Papa, I've been a bad girl. Would you switch me? I deserve it.' I tell you, I was so proud! I switched her good."

We listened incredulously for a few minutes more until the Voice of the Carolinas interrupted the preacher for a commercial. We retuned to the blandness of a light rock station.

* * *

The corporal punishment of children is a debated subject in the United States. In other parts of the developed world, the argument has been more or less settled: using corporal punishment against children, whether in school or at home is considered both morally wrong and unproductive. Corporal punishment teaches that the way to solve problems is to use violence. That is an unhelpful lesson. As nonviolentists we are opposed to any kind of physical punishment of children (in much the same way that we are opposed to any kind of physical punishment of spouses).

We have just made at least half of our readers uncomfortable. The sad truth is that causing physical pain to children is the most common experience of violence in our society. Parents hit their children often out of anger or frustration, sometimes to mask poor parenting skills, and sometimes from a mistaken belief that children are made good by physical pain. In the United States in a number of subcultures, and in some areas in the dominant culture, the physical punishment of children is seen as morally noble and essential for good parenting.

According to the Center for Effective Discipline, as of January 2014 thirty-six nations have outlawed corporal punishment in the home. One hundred and eighteen countries have abolished corporal punishment in schools. There is often fierce debate in the United States when suggestions are made to change the law regarding corporal punishment in public schools, and most states allow corporal punishment in private schools. In 2006 (the last recorded data) 223,190 incidences of corporal punishment occurred in United States public schools. This was an eighteen percent drop since the early 1980s (Center for Effective Discipline 2014b). That the trend is downward is a good sign. That almost a quarter of a million children are assaulted by teachers legally each year, most often with a wooden implement, remains a moral scandal and should cause outrage. It remains mostly hidden.

However, the violence and suffering children face in public schools is small compared to the physical assault children face in the home. So far legislators and the courts have been reluctant to oppose physical punishment by parents. The United States is not among the countries that have outlawed corporal punishment in the home (except for the state of Minnesota). Psychologist Michael Marshall demonstrates that, from a number of studies, in the United States parents severely assault 1.7 million children each year, 5.4 million children are struck each year with objects, and sixty percent of child abuse cases begin with physical punishment (2002, 13).

Perhaps part of the resistance to a government ban on spanking in the United States is a function of a resistance to anything the government might suggest. In some American political discourse, especially of the extreme political right, any government involvement in family life is too much government involvement. Might it be that those who lean this way politically see a prohibition on spanking to be one more unwarranted intrusion by government in the family? Pinker says that this view:

> . . . is consistent with other intrusions of the state into the family, such as compulsory schooling, mandatory vaccination, the removal of children from abusive homes, the imposition of lifesaving medical care over the objection of religious parents, and the prohibition of female genital cutting . . . (Pinker 2012, 437)

The phenomenon is not limited to the political right or libertarianism. We know of families who consider themselves left-leaning, or progressive, who object to state education and hence home school their children, and others who object to mandatory vaccination. Resistance to government seems to be in the DNA of many Americans, in a way that it is not for most Europeans. Those in Europe complain about governments, but it is usually in the context that the government has the right to, and ought to, fix things.

Worry about unwarranted government interference in family life is only a partial explanation as to why spanking persists in the United States. That parents have a right to treat their children as they see fit runs very deep. It is linked to the notion that a parent will always know what is best for their child, rather than a stranger. Parents often become uncomfortable if someone else tells them how to parent in better ways. Spanking persists, too, because the parent–child relationship is the last bastion of relational property ownership. Slavery was the first ownership issue to be settled. Human beings cannot morally own other people as if they were merely property. However, after the abolition of slavery the notion of male ownership of females persisted. The element of the traditional wedding service where the bride's father "gives away" the bride to the new male is a shadow of property ownership rights. The woman had no separate identity in law. This male privilege is the basis of spousal abuse. "She's mine," "My woman," "She needed teaching a lesson," are all rooted in the idea that the male owns the female and could do with her as he wished. It is why historically the husband could legally assault the wife—cause her physical pain—and the law turned a blind eye, in much the same way that the law now turns a blind eye to parents hitting their children. Sociologist Murray Straus terms this a "conspiracy of silence" (see his analysis, 2009.) The parent's comments "It doesn't really hurt!" "It was for the kid's own good!" "It's the only way the kid will learn!" are all echoes of the husband's "I didn't hurt her!" "It was for her own good!" and "It's the only way she'll learn!" Thankfully as a society we have developed, and spousal abuse (though still practiced on a large scale) no longer has an aura of sanctity. The spousal abuser is now frowned upon. The legal system is slowly moving in favor of the victim of domestic abuse.

We are changing, too, on our awareness of the violence that spanking causes to children, yet more slowly. There was a noticeable change in attitudes toward spanking from the 1960s through the early 1990s. When asked if you agree with the statement, "It is necessary to discipline a child with a good hard spanking," in 1968 there was an eighty-six percent approval rate. This had dropped to seventy-seven percent in 1975 (see Straus 2009, 20). However, in 2012, seventy-seven percent of men and sixty-five percent of women agreed with the statement (see Child Trends Data bank 2013, 2).

Murray Straus concludes:

- Almost every American child has been hit by his or her parents.
- Corporal punishment often begins in infancy. It climbs to a peak of at least 90 percent by ages three to four and then declines.
- Even in their late teens (ages 15–17), about a quarter of American children still experience some sort of corporal punishment (2009, 32).

However, there were important changes:

- The more severe types of corporal punishment declined sharply.
- Parents used corporal punishment less often—on children of all ages and both boys and girls.
- The decrease was greater for boys, but boys continue to be hit more than girls. (Straus 2009, 33)

However, whether there has been a decline in parents spanking their children, or a decline in parents owning up to the fact that they spank their children is impossible to say. The fact remains that violence against children in the form of spanking, either with the hand or with an implement, is still by far the most common everyday violence we face in our culture. While violence has declined in most all other areas of society, in childcare the move away from violence has been remorselessly slow.

Why do many people still think violence against our most vulnerable by those who care for them is still acceptable? One of the most common answers is that sometimes violence is the only way to bring about change. Spanking is a pragmatic way to turn wayward children into productive adults. Because the vast majority of children experience this type of violence, by implication the vast majority of children are then wayward. However, psychologists and sociologists make strong arguments why the pragmatic view is more like an urban myth than a scientific fact. Beside the immediate and direct harm of physical pain and bruising, the long-term effects on the child and on society are far reaching. Straus presents data that link corporal punishment with suicide, becoming an abuser of others, crime, and masochistic sex. Not all children who are spanked in turn become violent toward others. But, a culture that extolls the virtue of childcare through violence, is also a culture that seeks to solve its problems violently.

In chapter four, we looked at the ethical reasons why violence is unacceptable—violence ignores individual autonomy, causes harm, is unfair, does not do good, is based on false myths, strips those against whom it is used of their essential human dignity and equality, and does not work in the long run. Is spanking children an exception to these general ethical principles? Traditionally, children have not been counted as fully "human" as adults, in the same way that African slaves were not (ended in the nineteenth century) and women were not (ended in the early twentieth century). Slaves, women, and children were equally not given autonomy and respect—largely based on antiquated ideas about property and ownership. The exceptionalism given to the continued acceptance of using violence against the most vulnerable in our society is based on a shadow of this proprietary and patriarchal idea that children are not really people in the same way that adults are. If we grant to children full humanity, then we will not be able to use violence to "teach them a lesson," because, "it's the only way they will learn," or because "I've tried reasoning and it doesn't work."

* * *

Most summers we like to have at least a few days camping by the ocean. We are not "primitive campers"—no bathroom-free backwoods for us! But we do like the smell and feel of tenting, outdoor living, and relative freedom from technology. Tent walls are thin! We had nicely settled into camp and heard a little boy "playing up" a few tents away. He was part of a large family, mom and dad and six or seven children of varying ages. The mother tried reasoning with the boy for a few minutes. The father gave a warning. The little boy carried on. A few moments later we heard the steady "thwack" of wood on flesh as the boy was thoroughly paddled. He whimpered for a while. The mother and other children were silent.

Nonviolence Is Not the Same as No Discipline

"I do so admire your nonviolent parenting stance," the young mother said, but Darren and I are just about at our wits' end!" She began to cry softly.

Jane handed her a tissue, and Susan dabbed her tears.

"You see, I think some kids just need discipline. It might have worked with yours being loving and nonviolent, and not disciplining your kids. But ours . . . " She twisted the tissue between her fingers. "They're little monsters!"

As Jane pressed gently for further details of Susan and Darren's parenting style, it became obvious that they had interpreted nonviolence as "no boundaries, anything goes, no discipline at all," and the children were ruling the roost.

Earlier we looked at the historical ways philosophers have considered human nature. These views have permeated general culture in two popular ways of viewing the nature of children. In the first way, children are seen as barely more than wild animals, born unruly and needing to be tamed. Like a young wild stallion, the spirit of the child needs to be broken. Once broken, the adult can proceed to rebuild the child in a more civilized way. A child will not naturally be obedient to authority, and this must be forced on the child. This view has often been interpreted as needing corporal punishment, to teach the child a lesson. This view is still quite prevalent in parts of American culture, most particularly among the fundamentalist religious groups. One of the most notorious texts in the Bible with regard to childcare says, "Those who spare the rod of discipline hate their children!" (Proverbs 13:24) Those who take the Bible literally assume that God sanctions corporal punishment, often with a literal stick, or paddle. It goes even further, God *requires* corporal punishment for good parenting. This religious view is often accompanied by an image of God as a harsh regulator of human behavior. "God is not mocked," says a sign next to the mailbox of a house not far from us. "Be sure, your sins will find you out!" says another. At its worst this religious view is the type that protests outside a gay wedding ceremony, announcing the wrath of God, and hell for the newlyweds. Even at its best this religious view sees God is an intolerant father figure rather than a nurturing parent. If God is harsh and readily punishes, then shouldn't parents of disobedient children do the same?

The second way of looking at the human nature of children is broadly the opposite. This view says that children are not born like wild beasts to tame, but rather as little paragons of virtue. It is only though society, with its socialization and control, that children become bad. The best way to care for children is to leave them to their own devices, to allow their own creativity to shine through. Certainly, any corporal punishment would be frowned upon. Yet, in this view, any form of discipline is considered detrimental. No distinctions are made between using a hand or a paddle against a child and setting reasonable boundaries—both are seen as an infringement of the child's liberty to be creative.

* * *

"Would you like milk and sugar in your coffee, Shirley," Andy said, as he watched five-year-old Jason hit out with his fist at his mom.

"I want a cookie! I want a cookie!" Jason said as he tore at his mother's skirt.

Shirley ignored him and tried to engage in conversation. "Milk, no sugar, thanks . . . Ouch!"

Jason had taken more direct measures. He had kicked his mom in the shin—quite hard, if Shirley's cry of pain was anything to go by.

To Andy's amazement Shirley did nothing, besides rubbing her shin. The conversation did not get very far as Jason's tantrum reached new decibels, and his assault on his mother continued unabated. After a while, Shirley made a feeble excuse and withdrew to the comparative safety of her car. As she strapped Jason into the back seat he managed a rather deft kick to Shirley's stomach, just as the buckle of the seat belt clicked into place.

Jason had never known any boundaries. Discipline was an alien word to Shirley. She had once read a book on childcare that advocated total freedom for children. "Jason is special," she had once told us. "He's not like other children." We felt deeply sorry for Shirley. Her life for the next thirteen or fourteen years would likely be close to hell.

Should she have spanked Jason? Perhaps at least told him that his violence was not acceptable? Should she have kicked him back (as some suggest) to teach him not to kick others?

* * *

Over the years, we have noticed that children whose parents choose not to provide clear boundaries—helping their children learn self-discipline—are children who are often willing to inflict pain on others. It is not a direct correlation, but pretty close. In Shirley's case, it was often pain inflicted on her, though we heard when Jason later attended school he was quite a bully. Children who have not been taught self-discipline are more likely to hurt other children. The reason is clear: they have never learned to keep their impulses and urges in control. But to learn self-control does not require spanking or violence.

* * *

We were in a local park with some good friends of ours. Their little boy was playing with our two foster children. A dispute arose over the toy with which they all wanted to play. Voices were raised and our friend's boy began to assault physically one of the foster children. Our little one was being hurt. "Oh, leave them to it," the father said. "I don't believe in intervening in children's squabbles."

However, Andy did! He quickly, and authoritatively separated the boys, stepping between them, preventing flailing arms from making contact, but without hurting them. The boy's father was not pleased, and sadly we lost a friend. From our perspective, it was simply not acceptable that, under the guise of freedom and creativity, a child should be allowed to hurt other children. Being a nonviolentist, Andy did not use violence, but nor did he allow the violence of the child to continue. Nonviolence is about reducing violence in any given situation.

* * *

Must we choose either the discipline of the paddle or the chaos of no boundaries? No! There is an alternative. It is to refuse violence against children, but to insist on careful boundaries in which children can learn the social skills needed to become decent and responsible adults.

There are two unhelpful "myths" about discipline that need to be countered. The first is that discipline is a bad thing. The second, is that discipline is the same as punishment.

Discipline comes from the root word meaning "learner." A disciple is one who learned from a teacher. In the parental context, children become self-disciplined and self-controlled by learning from the boundaries that parents set for them. When children are very small, the boundaries are set with little explanation to the children. But very soon children respond to being told why to eat the dog food is a bad thing, or why to walk into the road without looking for cars is a bad practice.

As we have considered, this requires helping children develop the twin faculties of empathy and self-discipline—learning to feel as others feel, and so to care for them, and learning to control their own inner urges toward harming others. A large part of this process is for parents to model empathy and self-discipline for their children.

That the words "discipline" and "punishment" have come to mean the same thing in popular usage has not been helpful. Our loving nonviolent home is very much a disciplined environment—helping children to live within healthy boundaries by learning self-discipline— but not an environment of punishment, with its close association with painful measures.

Setting Boundaries

Setting boundaries is hard for children who have been neglected and socialized with few or no boundaries to their behavior. Many of the children we have cared for have often run wild and been left to their own devises. Regular bedtime hours, sitting at a table for mealtimes, getting up in the morning for school, personal hygiene issues, respecting the boundaries of others' bodies and possessions are new to them. Yet harder than the outer, physical boundaries are the emotional ones.

* * *

Linda and her baby sister came to live with us after having been neglected and abused physically and sexually. Linda was pretty, with tight red curls, and a sweet smile, head often winsomely tilted to one side. However, she had no boundaries. Though only three years old she approached strangers in a way not usually seen in small children. At the checkout line in the local food store she turned to the man behind us and started rubbing her hand up and down his leg. The action was clearly learned sexualized behavior. We were fairly sure that Linda did not know what she was doing—merely copying something she had seen, or had happened to her. The man was clearly embarrassed and made a joke of it, but still it was a tricky situation to negotiate. At least part of us wanted to say in justification, "She's not really our child. We're just her foster carers. She must have picked that up somewhere else." Of course, we couldn't say so (however true it was) and politely excused ourselves.

* * *

The boundaries we set within the home are not many or burdensome. Mostly they are about building good habits regarding self and others. They include regular bedtimes ensuring sufficient sleep; the privacy and sanctity of bodies; absolutely not hitting or other forms of violence; no name calling or verbal abuse or insults; truth-telling, but not tale-telling; no foul or abusive language; regularity of mealtimes, avoiding the "drip feed" or "grazing" approach to food; personal hygiene and keeping clean. In many respects, these are obvious and basic. However, children who have only known the chaos of anything goes—or the violent response to unclear rules—have never internalized boundaries within which empathy and self-control can be developed.

When It All Goes Wrong

We have taken children into our home who challenge our nonviolent intentions. Some children test us because they have not known any other way of adult behavior. They behave in the way modeled for them. The adults in their life, so far, have responded to difficulties or challenges by verbal and physical violence. When these children feel threatened they mirror their caregivers. When Dejohn in the past annoyed or challenged his mother, mom screamed at him, called him names, and threatened him. Then if he continued to annoy, or disrespect her, mom would lash out. Dejohn would experience more or less pain, depending where her hand, or hairbrush, or anything else close to hand, caught him.

Children soon learn that in such a violent atmosphere, the correct approach is to posture violently. The adult screams, you scream back. The adult calls you names. You call names back. The adult lashes out. You lash out back. For many children violence has become a deeply ingrained pattern. When faced with calm, but firm, nonviolent forms of communication, the child's only response is a violent one.

For some parents, physical or sexual violence is the only way they communicate with the child. The little girl, in time, begins to confuse this type of attention with love. "My dad loves me. My dad hurts me. To love me is to hurt me."

When children come to us, we want to break the cycle of punishment and violence. If violence is all a child has known, loving nonviolence can be confusing at first. Here is a more or less verbatim encounter. The language is no exaggeration; this is what foster carers face.

* * *

Thirteen-year-old Desiree came home from school in a bad mood. Apparently, Ms. Bell had removed the MP3 player Desiree was not supposed to have at school. She had sneaked it out in her book bag. This was a repeated pattern. At home and at school Desiree chose her own path irrespective of others. She had learned to get her own way by acting out with tantrums. She frequently threatened and sometimes used violence. Her birth mom seemed powerless to prevent the abuse Desiree meted out to her. She frequently bullied other children at school, and the school principal was at the point of giving in and asking her to be removed to a more secure setting. Desiree had come to us as a last attempt to try to break the cycle of violence she had spiraled into.

"Ms. Bell had told you many times that your music player is not allowed in class," said Jane. "We've tried to tell you that there are consequences for actions. Anyway she said you could have it back at the end of the week."

"But I wanted it! I wanted to listen to music in class," Desiree responded. "It's my iPod not hers . . . She's no right to take it . . . I hate her . . . I told her to fuck herself."

Desiree had a way of working herself into a bad mood, muttering to herself as much as to anyone else.

"Anyway dinner's ready now," Andy said lightly, trying to divert the subject.

We had learned that to try to tackle the issue when she was in her mood would not work, but only escalate matters.

"I don't want dinner. I want my iPod" she said beginning now to shout.

"Well, let's have dinner and talk about it afterward."

"I don't want dinner. I hate you too!" she said, getting even louder.

"I'm sorry you feel that way," said Jane. "It's not the end of the world. Come on, after dinner we can watch a movie together."

"I don't wanna watch the fucking movie!" Desiree screamed.

"Desiree, you know shouting doesn't get us anywhere."

"Shut up you mother fucker! Get out of my face! I'm gonna kill Ms. Bell. I'm gonna take a knife and stab her. Then I'm gonna stab you too, you fucking whore . . ."

Desiree picked up the pepper pot and threw it across the kitchen. It smashed on the wall. Her screaming and violent behavior scared the dogs. Tail between their legs the little pugs cowered under the kitchen chairs. Desiree stormed out of the room, slamming the door.

For the next half hour Desiree returned to the kitchen screaming more verbal abuse and goading us into some kind of violent response.

Some time later, she came downstairs, red-faced from crying.

"I'm sorry I said those horrible things. I didn't mean to scare the dogs. I'm sorry."

* * *

How do foster carers feel when kids have out of control tantrums? We always feel emotionally bruised, sometimes angry, often inadequate, always questioning. Should we have done something differently. Did we miss a trigger? Was there an underlying issue we had missed? Sometimes you simply feel that you can take no more.

One response is to say that as nonviolence has not worked, we ought to spank the child. If all else fails use violence. Children should not get away with the behavior we suffered from Desiree. However, the data show that in such situations violence is ineffective in producing the desired change in children. The strong hand might solve an immediate problem. It might literally beat the child into submission. But, in terms of producing empathy and self-control in the child it is ineffective.

* * *

"I think you need to be away from the other children for a while, John," Andy said as two of the younger children tried to hold back tears after being hit by their older sibling.

"I'm not going and you can't make me," John replied belligerently.

"I think you ought to go now to calm down for a while. Then you can apologize to Kristy and Kaitlin for hurting them," Andy continued in a soft and sad tone.

John pushed his chair back roughly, scratching its legs on the wood floor. He pushed past Andy who banged against the tabletop.

"OK. Now you really need to take some time to calm down."

John turned abruptly and edged almost chest to chest with Andy.

"Go on! Hit me! You know you want to!" John mocked. "You're too weak to do it. You fucking coward! I've knocked over a three hundred pound guy before!"

Andy walked away, needing time to center, knowing that to face up to John at this point would be to resort to an alpha male stand-off, with much posturing. Jane intervened and defused the situation. John left the room cursing. In time, he began to learn to control his impulses, but it was a long struggle.

* * *

The "face-off" with a child is very difficult to deal with, more so the older the child. Usually, with children under twelve the easiest strategy is to prevent the face off before it occurs. Standing one's ground and asking the child to be alone for a while, or distracting them, often works with the younger child.

Teens are harder. Often, being physically bigger, the larger teenager could do real harm to us, to others, to themselves, and to property. On occasion, we have had a teenager completely out of control throwing things around a room and causing substantial damage. In such cases, when it is too late to defuse the situation before it gets out of hand, the priority is safety. If there are other children in the home, we make sure they go to a different physical space, outside of harm's way. If the dogs are present, we take them to a different room. We stay with the raging child, keeping a safe distance from flying objects, or fists and feet. In most cases the rage does not last too long, and the teen will exhaust herself.

Very sadly, we have cared for children where trust has broken down so completely, with rages occurring daily, that we have requested that the child be removed. On the few occasions when this has happened, the child has moved to another foster home (less likely) or to a more secure placement.

Of those who have moved to other loving nonviolent foster homes, we have seen a child turn things around. The new home does not see the same behaviors. In those cases we like to think that, even though with us things did not work out, the child had internalized at least something of value. We are always happy for some other re-parents to try just one more time.

We are less happy when the child leaves us for what is euphemistically called a "higher level of care." The more secure placement will likely give its staff the ability to restrain an out-of-control teen. This is violent. On those occasions where a child has left us for such a placement, we are deeply saddened. In the time with us we have not helped the child internalize nonviolence; his empathy and self-control remain weak. The "higher placement" will likely not teach empathy and self-control. The young person will be institutionalized, managed, restricted, and controlled, often through drugs, but also through violence when "necessary."

It would seem that nonviolence in those cases did not work. But, as a society we fool ourselves if we think that violence works better. In those cases we have failed the child we sought to help. Sadly, that is far too often the reality.

10

Loving Nonviolent Habits and Virtues

Recall that the Neo-Aristotelian way of looking at ethics is not about rules and regulations. It seeks to answer the question, "How shall we live?" To begin to answer the question we need to take notice of our values—those things we hold most dear. When we understand our values, they in turn suggest a *telos*—a goal or purpose—that we choose to pursue. When the goal is internalized, a Neo-Aristotelian asks what kind of person is most likely to achieve that goal? The type of person you are demonstrates what virtues—character traits—you have that make you that type of person. For our purposes, a loving nonviolent person is someone who has the virtues of loving nonviolence. The very practical question then becomes: and how does anyone develop virtues? The very practical answer is by habituation. Build the habit of loving nonviolence through many little loving and nonviolent actions and, in time, you become a loving nonviolent person—effectively we are what we repeatedly do. One act of loving nonviolence does not make for a loving nonviolent person. But someone who acts lovingly and nonviolently repeatedly day after day becomes a loving nonviolent person.

Building habits is neither a "quick fix," nor an easy road to walk. We have been building the habits of nonviolence for over thirty years, and some days it feels like we are just beginning! Intention is important, as are baby steps rather than large leaps. Daily practice is the norm. Examples abound from playing a musical instrument, to learning to drive a car, to learning how to quilt. All are learned by practice. If you want to acquire the virtue of tightrope walking, you will need the habit of getting on the wire every day. And falling off. And getting back on again. This requires intentionality and commitment. To become a loving nonviolent re-parent also requires intentionality and commitment.

To apply this to foster carers and adopters, let's try to summarize what we are saying. The values we have as carers are derived in part from our own upbringing, our life experiences, and our encounters with life generally. But, they are derived in part negatively. We have seen what happens to children when they are neglected, maltreated, or abused. We see fearfulness, mistrust, hatred, willingness to cause others harm, violence, depression, and anxiety. We realize this ought not to be, and so we form values that are the opposites of that which has been a part of the child's life to date. If a child has observed and experienced violence, then the counter to that experience would be to value nonviolence, or nonharm. If a child has experienced mistrust, then we learn to value trustfulness. When a child has been subject to hate, then the countervalue to hatred would be love.

We have suggested that when we uncover our values (derived positively from our experiences of life, and negatively from observing the suffering children endure) then we can choose a purpose that matches with our most deeply held values. That purpose we suggest is loving nonviolent re-parenting.

We looked, then, at this process slightly differently, suggesting that we form a sense of moral purpose through the process of conscientization, internalization, and intentionalization. That is, what we feel, what we think, and how we choose to act. We have our feelings awakened to the plight of children, we seriously think about that plight, and we choose to act on our reflections. Again, we suggest that such a process leads to the life purpose of loving nonviolent re-parenting.

Verbs and Nouns

When we were at grade school we learned that verbs are "doing words." We learned that nouns are "naming words . . . a person, a place, a feeling, or a thing." We have since learned that syntax is a little more complex than that, but this is a useful handle for us to think about virtues and habits. A virtue is a "thing." A habit is something you do. So we might say that a virtue is a thing of which a habit is an action. If this is true then, for example, love is both a thing and an action. Love is what I want to see in myself, and in my relationships. But "to love," to do the action of loving, is the habit that will produce love. Love is a noun and a verb. This is true for all virtues and habits. Every virtue has a corresponding habit.

What, then, are the virtues and corresponding habits of loving nonviolent re-parenting? We are relying here on work Andy did in writing his book, *Love as a Guide to Morals* (2012). In that book Andy suggests twelve virtues of love with their corresponding habits. The twelve are not an exhaustive list, nor a definitive one. Readers could come up with a different set of virtues and habits. These are rather *something like* the character traits needed by foster carers and adopters if they are to pursue the goal of loving nonviolent re-parenting.

While each pair of virtues/habits is important on its own, the sum is more than the parts. The foster carer who develops these virtues and habits will become a loving nonviolent person who will most likely function according to them in any given situation. Of course, there is no guarantee that this will be the case. Circumstances and pressures sometimes cause people to do things outside of their character. The normally placid person may be pushed so hard through the circumstances of life that she explodes with rage one day. "I'm not like that," she says. "That was so out of character for her," a friend responds. We make this type of comment because we do see the sense in talking about character. To do something "out of character" is noteworthy because most of us act "in character" most of the time. It is the "in character" that we are concerned about here. How do we develop those habits and virtues that will make it so most of the time we act in character as loving nonviolent re-parents?

Here is our list of the virtues of loving nonviolent re-parenting:

- Goodness (beneficence)
- Nonharm (non-maleficence, ahimsa)
- Fidelity (faithfulness)
- Reparation with forgiveness
- Fairness (equality, justice)
- Respect with mindfulness
- Gratefulness
- Care
- Courage
- Kindness with gentleness
- Moderation
- Nonpossessiveness

Here is the list of corresponding habits:

- Doing good
- Not harming
- Keeping faith
- Repairing wrongs and forgiving
- Treating fairly and equally
- Respecting with attentiveness
- Being thankful
- Caring

- Being courageous
- Acting kindly and gently
- Acting moderately
- Not possessing

Unpacking the Virtues and Habits

Below we make some brief comments on these habits and virtues.

Goodness—Doing Good

The first virtue/habit is that of goodness and doing good. The technical term for this is "beneficence," but we tend not to use that in everyday speech. Its meaning—to seek good and not ill for others—is a primary virtue of loving nonviolent re-parenting; although it is quite difficult at times to know what is "good." In our context we mean the flourishing of children we care for, especially their flourishing in relationships. It is not merely an individualistic idea. As we develop the habit of always seeking the best for others, we develop the virtue of goodness. If we love the children in our care, we will want them to flourish. In other words, their well-being is our intention.

Intention is not fool proof. Sometimes we can act with the best of intentions, yet the result is not what we had anticipated. There is always a risk that even when we intend the child's good, we get it wrong. Doubtless, even with a good intention we still think about the potential consequences of our actions. Yet, consequences are uncertain.

This highlights three very important ideas that spring from moral philosophy. The first is acting according to what Immanuel Kant (1724–1804) called a "good will." In some respects though we can't be responsible for consequences that are unseen, we are always responsible for our intention to act in a beneficent way. Second, is that we still do need to think about possible outcomes of our actions. We need to "weigh up" the potential consequences for good or ill. This follows the thinking of John Stuart Mill (1806–1873) that consequences matter. Third, is that even when we have given it our best shot to think about consequences, at the moment of choice we take a risk. This is something like SørenKierkegaard's (1813–1855) "leap to faith."

Taken together this suggests that we need to intend the good for the children in our care, that we consider the possible consequences of actions, and that we take the risk and make our best decision. If this process becomes a habit—intention, consequences, action—with regard to beneficence, then in time the habit of good actions will tend to make us good people. That is true for all the virtues and habits we consider below.

Nonharm—Refusing Violent Actions

The matching virtue to beneficence is nonmaleficence—nonharm. In Sanskrit the word for nonharm is *ahimsa*, and was beloved of Mohandas K. Gandhi. Literally it means the avoidance of violence, and is a very full concept. In Gandhi's use ahimsa would cover both beneficence and nonmaleficence, as two sides of the same coin. This idea reaches to the heart of what we understand the task of foster caring to be as loving nonviolent re-parents. In a sense, we have covered already much of what nonviolence is, but we wanted to include it as a virtue with its corresponding habits. It would be difficult to be violent in some aspects of life, and then to try to switch to nonviolence in the care of children. To be lovingly nonviolent in our care of children requires that we develop the habits of nonviolence in the whole of life. Then our loving nonviolent care of children will simply be an outflow of who we are at a deep existential level.

To develop the virtue of nonviolence through the habits of nonviolence requires us to learn something of nonviolent conflict resolution. In this regard we commend again the work of Marshall Rosenberg and nonviolent communication as an excellent tool to think through issues of nonviolence (2003, 2005a, 2005b).

Courage—Acting Courageously

Foster carers and adopters need courage in abundance! Courage is often thought of as a martial, probably masculine, virtue. It might seem to be the antithesis of loving nonviolence. While Aristotle includes courage in his list of the virtues for a well-lived life, he finds no place for loving nonviolence. His context was very masculinist, patriarchal, and martial. In this book, our approach is quite different and this is one of the reasons we speak of Neo-Aristotelianism. We take our cue from Aristotle, but part company with him over some fundamental issues of what a well-lived life might look like.

However, loving nonviolence, like war, requires courage. It is a common misunderstanding that nonviolence is the choice of the weak and soft. Strong people need courage to use violence, so the story goes. We think it is the reverse! Nonviolence is closely associated with pacifism. A common mistake is to think of pacifism as "passivism." Our culture values action over no-action. The person of action is praised.

The passive person is considered weak. However, pacifism is the desire for peaceful solutions to conflict rather than violent ones. Pacifists are most often quite active rather than passive in their search for peace. Gandhi, for instance, required thorough training in nonviolence equal to any training a soldier in the army needs. He assumed that to become nonviolent sometimes required the *satyagrahi* (his term for those who followed *satyagraha*, "truth force" or "love force") to absorb the violence of an aggressor into themselves. In other words, loving nonviolence is willing to suffer, absorb and, ultimately, end violence. Nonetheless, it's easy to see how because of the connection of nonviolence to pacifism, that nonviolence might be considered a weak choice. However, to always make a choice for love requires as much courage as to make a choice for violence.

Courage is required, often, in other than life and death situations. Loving nonviolence runs the risk of rejection or failure. To face failure or rejection raises powerful emotions. Sometimes failure is such an unbearable prospect that we might rather not try than to suffer the consequences of rejection or failure. More than a few friends have commented to us that they would not choose to become foster carers. "I couldn't possibly face it if the kid rejected me," said a good friend of Jane's. "And what must it be like when you get really attached to a kid and then they move on somewhere else. I couldn't bear it." To care requires courage. Courage is only required when the possibility of being hurt is real. Over the years we have faced many hurts. But, you carry on, and that requires courage.

Justice—Acting Fairly

Many of us become foster carers because of an injustice we perceive has happened to children. Justice is a complex concept and is much more than criminal justice, which is only one aspect of the much broader picture of justice. We might simplify justice (following philosopher John Rawls, 1921–2002) as fairness. When you first hear the stories of neglected children, instinctively you think, "But that's not fair!" These children did nothing to deserve the treatment they received at the hands of adults who ought to have known better. Fairness is an idea we pick up very early in our lives. Take any sibling group and begin to pour soda into glasses. Fill one three-quarters full and the others only half. At least one little voice will announce, "But that's not fair! She's got more than me." Fairness is closely linked with equality. For the children, fairness means something like "equal shares." But equal shares is not the only way to look at fairness. It might mean giving a child what the child needs to succeed rather than strictly equal shares. In life, some children are given a larger share of important goods—love, safety, security, material things—than other children. Children who come into the foster care system are usually among the "have nots." They have not received a fair share with other children. In some regards, foster care is an attempt to right that wrong, to provide a fair attempt at life for children who have missed out so far.

Yet, popularly, love and justice are sometimes perceived as opposites. Look at the criminal justice system: there is no love there. Justice is not about love, it is about the rightness or wrongness of actions. Perhaps strangely, it is said that both justice and love are blind. Justice is blind because justice acts impartially. Love is blind because the lover refuses to see the faults of her loved ones.

How then can justice be a virtue of loving nonviolence? Foster carers seek fairness for their children. They care for their children impartially regardless of the faults they see in the children. In that sense the justice of loving nonviolence is "blind" because it seeks fairness impartially, but at the same time it is clear-sighted and is open to see the faults and imperfections of others, while refusing to judge them.

Kindness with Gentleness—Acting Kindly and Gently

Kindness with gentleness is perhaps an obvious virtue of loving nonviolence. It is easy to see why foster carers ought to act kindly and gently, and become in time kind and gentle people.

In *Love as A Guide to Morals*, Andy gives a definition of kindness as:

> That virtue of showing consideration, generosity and open-heartedness to others. Kindness is very soft, perhaps the most tender of love's virtues. Kindness as an action is love in motion toward the Other in tenderness to reduce the distance between lover and Other in a warm and mild way. (2012, 99)

Many of the children we have cared for have known kindness only in sporadic ways. This is why it is such an important virtue and why the habit of acting kindly is imperative. Some writers go so far as to think that kindness alone is sufficient to guide our lives. Kindness helps reduce friction. It helps relationships run smoothly. It's hard to think of anyone not being warmed, or surprised, or made happy, by kindness. To think of kind actions, even to act kindly toward another, makes you smile. Kindness is a contributing factor toward our own and the child's well-being.

We link kindness with gentleness and though they are closely related they are not the same.

> Kindness will always be gentle, but whereas kindness is the action itself, gentleness is the manner in which all actions should be carried out. So, it is appropriate to say "kind and gentle." (Fitz-Gibbon 2012, 99)

One day, your child is playing on a swing in the local playground. She falls bruising and scraping her knees. You act kindly toward the child as you help her to her feet and ask if she is okay. But, the manner you carry out your action is with gentleness. You can see the difference when we talk about a gentle wind, but never speak of a kind wind. Loving nonviolence is to practice acts of kindness in a gentle manner. Foster care is always to be kind and gentle.

Care—Caring For

It might seem obvious, but care is also a virtue for the foster carer! Just as some writers see kindness as an overarching and sufficient basis for a moral life, others see care as just such an all-embracing practice.

The feminist philosophy of care is, perhaps, the most important work so far in this regard. In philosophy, from the early 1980s, a new way of thinking about ethics came from feminist philosophy (we have already considered the work of Sara Ruddick in chapter five). These philosophers challenged traditionally western liberal views of morality as too masculinist in emphasis. They noted that, historically, males had carried out most public ethical thinking. In the process, this biased ethical ideas toward concerns and interests that belonged to men. As men tended to be concerned with issues outside the home, and women with those things relating to the home and the care of children, ethics became biased in that direction. Issues such as contracts, and rights, and justice became prominent. Women's lives were more concerned with nurture, relationships, and with care. Women's issues were not considered as ethically important as men's. These feminist philosophers urged a rethink about care as central to the ethical task. Needless to say, this virtue of care is close to the heart of what it means to be a loving nonviolent re-parent.

The associated habit of the virtue of care is "caring for." Feminist philosopher and ethicist of care Nel Noddings makes a useful distinction between "caring about" and "caring for." The habit of caring is not merely caring about the plight of maltreated children. Ask any sensitive person and likely as not they will say that they, too, care about what happens to children. However, the habit of "caring for" is the day to day, mundane, courageous work that re-parents carry out for children who have known violence.

Faithfulness—Keeping Faith With

Many of the children who come into care have not been kept faith with. They have been let down again and again. Their level of trust is often very low. When adults say things, they tend not to mean them. Adults in their lives have made promises and have broken them.

Perhaps strangely, many children exercise extraordinary faithfulness toward their birth parents even when they are abusers. We hear constantly, "My mom really loves me," "My dad didn't mean to hurt me," and "I still love my mom!" Older children count the moments until they can return home. Another form of faithfulness is a wall of silence. Children who have been maltreated or neglected are often unwilling to talk about it. To do so would be to see a betrayal of their family. It has amazed us that the children who have been betrayed often remain faithful to the betrayers.

It seems all the more important that foster carers, then, need to develop a level of faithfulness toward the children in their care. If we demonstrate faithfulness to our children, then they will be more willing to trust us. Trust takes time to build and can be broken very quickly. When children and teens come to us, we give them a lot of trust. We tell them we will trust them until they do something to break that trust.

Teens often want to go to the shopping mall to be with friends. That, of course, excludes our being there. We generally agree, unless the caseworker has given us good reasons for not allowing the teen at the mall unsupervised—previous disruptive behavior or stealing are the usual red flags. We set a time to be home. Most teens respect the rule, but some do not. If the teen returns several hours after the set home time we tell them that trust is broken, but that we will give them another opportunity to rebuild. After a second time we generally give them the "This is not OK. Three strikes and you're out!" If the teen abuses the trust three times, then the trips to the mall alone no longer happen. We continue to talk about trust and the need to rebuild it with us. After a week or two we usually get the plea, "Please can I go? Everyone else goes . . ." And we try again, usually with a shorter time.

"Thank you! Thank you! I won't be late. I promise!" cries the delighted teen. It has happened often that the few weeks at home works and the teen returns at the agreed time, pleased with themselves. Trust is gradually rebuilt. It is patient work and takes time and energy on the part of the foster carer.

Trust needs to be built both ways. The child who has been let down many times by adults will hardly dare trust another adult. The message they have received is that "adults can't be trusted." We are careful not to promise anything we can't deliver. When we make a promise we ensure that we fulfill it. This requires a high level of honesty and integrity on the part of the carer. Sometimes it is easier to resolve a difficulty with a rash promise. It is a foolish strategy that sometimes backfires in the short term and always backfires in the long term.

Each day brings opportunities to be faithful. Each new situation is a challenge for trust to take place.

Forgiveness with Reparation: Forgiving Wrongs and Fixing Mistakes

In our culture we have inherited a strong emphasis on forgiveness from a shared Judeo-Christian past. Hence, forgiveness is often associated with a religious impulse. The religious emphasis of forgiveness, in turn, is that I, the "sinner," need to be forgiven for my wrongs. It is about my escape from personal badness. Children who have been subjected to a strong religious upbringing have often been given a reinforcement of a very negative view of the self. We have sometimes thought of it as the "miserable worm" view of the self—the self as utterly bad, always in need of forgiveness. To socialize children in that way is not helpful. It is not what we mean by the virtue of forgiveness.

Forgiveness, as a virtue, is the letting go of wrongs, real and perceived. It is about the process of bringing reconciliation when relationships go wrong. Forgiveness means that offense will not destroy a relationship. It has helped us to think of forgiveness psychologically and relationally.

Psychologically, forgiveness is about the one offended letting go of the offense and freeing herself from bitterness and brooding. This is true when offense was intended and when no offense was intended. It is the one who perceives offense who suffers. Forgiveness allows that person to move on and exercise love again. In this sense, forgiveness is about the one forgiving and is not about the one forgiven. If someone wrongs you, and you continue to brood on the wrong, then the only person you hurt is yourself. Forgiveness frees you from inner self-harm.

However, forgiveness is also an important component of healthy relationships. When a genuine wrong has occurred forgiveness makes room for reconciliation. A wrong acts like a dark cloud that spoils a relationship. When you exercise the virtue of forgiveness and communicate it to the wrongdoer, the relationship has space to grow again. Both parties benefit. Yet, relational forgiveness does require some change on the part of the one being forgiven. If forgiveness of wrongs is too easily given, nothing is learned. Children need to learn to say sorry when they have caused harm; and this must be part of the process before forgiveness is extended. Actions that harm have consequences. Wrongs must be righted where possible. It's a difficult but important lesson.

For foster carers psychological forgiveness and relational forgiveness are equally important. When a cared-for child hurts or abuses a carer (using words or fists) it is vitally important to build the habit of letting go of wrongs. For their own mental and emotional well-being the carer needs to learn to let go and forgive wrongs quickly. Equally, for the sake of the child, the child needs to right the wrong where possible—perhaps an expression of sorrow—but then needs to hear words of forgiveness. "Sally, you really hurt me when you kicked me. I'm glad you have said sorry. Let's move on. Of course I still love you!"

Mindfulness, Gratefulness, Nonpossessiveness: Acting Mindfully, Saying Thank You, Letting Go

We consider mindfulness more fully in the next chapter as one of the ways to care for ourselves. Here we consider it as essential for the children in our care. Mindfulness includes awareness, or attentiveness. It is the way we are present for our children, giving them our attention, truly "hearing" them.

Part of mindfulness is to be in the present moment without either being locked into the past or the future. With our children, if I am focused on what happened between us in the past, it will hinder good communication and relationship in the present. If we are thinking constantly of what might happen next, then we are not truly present for the child just now. The habit of mindfulness requires daily attention. It is a moment-by-moment focus when we are with our children.

At times this is difficult, especially when children are very demanding. To give attention to a child when the same question is asked for the fourth or fifth time requires patience. The temptation is simply to switch off. Mindfulness requires presence.

This leads to our next virtue, that of gratefulness—a simple though extraordinarily rich idea. Gratefulness is a reminder to celebrate with joy all the goodness of life. It is a very happy virtue. Being thankful for who we are, and for everything we have, frees us to love the children in our care. It is linked closely to nonpossessiveness.

To grip too tightly those we love is a real temptation. Yet the too tight grip spoils love. Foster carers and adopters (as all parents) need to practice letting go. Carers need to give their children space to grow and be themselves. It is the case supremely for parents as their children mature. It is the parent's failure to let go of the late-teenager that is a cause of so much friction. But, how hard it is to do! That is why all virtues require small steps. In letting-go of our children by increasing their freedom—at first in small things and then in larger—the parent gradually gets used to letting go.

This is one of the great insights of Buddhist philosophy. In Buddhism's Four Noble Truths, the problem with life is that life is a life of suffering. Attachment is the cause of suffering. To be freed from suffering is to let go of attachments. Much Buddhist practice is learning the way of nonattachment and letting-go.

Moderation—Acting Moderately

Moderation is a foremost Aristotelian virtue. Aristotle was very keen to avoid excesses and deficiencies. The best life was a life lived in the "golden mean"—neither too much nor too little of anything. We might call this a life of balance. As a virtue, balance is paramount for carers.

Many children in care have never known moderation or balance in their lives. Birth parents have often been excessive in punishment, in substance abuse, or in food consumption. They have been deficient in loving care, in affirmation, or in kind words. Children who have been neglected have known great deficiency.

* * *

"Karrie, you have eaten enough! I can see you are struggling to finish the food on your plate. You know, it's okay to leave some."

"No, no, no!" screamed Karrie, working herself into a tantrum. "You are not stealing my food."

Karrie had never learnt moderation in anything. She had never had moderation modeled for her. As her foster carers we began to model moderation, explaining why we chose smaller portions, and why we left food sometimes.

* * *

Caring can be so intense that foster carers need the virtue of moderation to prevent excess and burnout. Moderation was a primary virtue for the ancient Greeks—especially the Stoics. To allow yourself to get "too high" would likely result in a great crash down. To allow yourself to wallow in the depths would make it all the more difficult to find balance in life. The Stoic philosopher Epictetus said:

> Of all existing things some are in our power, and others are not in our power. In our power are thought, impulse, will to get and will to avoid, and, in a word, everything which is our own doing. Things not in our power include the body, property, reputation, office, and, in a word, everything which is not our own doing. Things in our power are by nature free, unhindered, untrammeled; things not in our power are weak, servile, subject to hindrance, dependent on others. Remember then that if you imagine that what is naturally slavish is free, and what is naturally another's is your own, you will be hampered, you will mourn, you will be put to confusion, you will blame gods and men; but if you think that only your own belongs to you, and that what is another's is indeed another's, no one will ever put compulsion or hindrance on you, you will blame none, you will accuse none, you will do nothing against your will, no one will harm you, you will have no enemy, for no harm can touch you. (*The Enchiridion*)

In short, only be concerned about those things that you can control. In a life of balance, there is much that the foster carer can do nothing about, nor fix—the past and all experiences the child has had before coming into care, and the future that cannot be known or controlled. To dwell over much on these things produces only heartache and can lead to depression. Better to find a balanced life and be concerned about those things we can most immediately affect. We continue to look at caring for ourselves in the next chapter.

The Care of All Sentient Beings: Vegetarianism

When children first arrive, we welcome them into our kitchen. In the winter months, more often than not, there is a friendly log fire blazing in the hearth. In the summer, usually, we will sit on the deck in our back yard. For administrative and practical reasons, children often arrive late in the afternoon. Their arrival is often accompanied by the smell of cooking. We offer the caseworker a cup of tea and then we have our first chat.

"So, Jane, can you tell Angeleek what the rules of the home are?" said the caseworker

"To be honest we don't have many," Jane replied, looking at Angeleek with a smile. "But here's one—No girls in boys rooms." Angeleek looks down at her shoes, a little embarrassed.

"And we don't do physical violence," Andy joins in. "That means no hitting each other. Also, we try to be kind to each other with our words. That means we don't raise our voices, if we can at all help it. We don't shout at each other, or call each other names."

"That's because we are a nonviolent home," continued Jane.

The caseworker, who has known us for a while and has brought a number of children to us, said, "But, tell Angeleek the big rule."

"Ah, you mean that we are vegetarians?" Jane replied. She smiled again at the young girl. "We don't eat anything that had a face, as Linda McCartney used to say."

Angeleek looked up from her shoes to the caseworker, a look of pleading in her eyes. "No meat. I think I'll die! What can I eat?"

Angeleek didn't die, and in a very short time she came to enjoy the variety of vegetarian cuisine. When we go to a restaurant, Angeleek often chose the meat she craved. In time, the craving lessened and she became happy with vegetarianism, often choosing a none-meat dish for herself.

But not all children are as compliant as Angeleek. Many American children have been fed the lie—along with their Big Macs—that a large amount of meat is essential for a healthy diet. Meat eating, particularly for boys, becomes a point of pride. Some of our foster children have gone out of their way to tell animal cruelty stories, just to "get a rise" from us. We have learnt not to play.

Rather ours is a low-key refusal to be involved in the gross cruelty to animals that is the factory farming industry. When children ask us why we do not eat meat, we share stories from Farm Sanctuary and other compassionate organizations that care for animals. In the summer months we make at least one trip to Farm Sanctuary at Watkins Glen, New York—we have supported the organization for many years—to allow our foster children to meet the animals we sponsor: the pig (Shirley, who passed on, and then Terrin), the sheep (Donna), and lots of turkeys. Giving children exposure to living, sentient, playful beings, rather than meat on a plate, helps children develop empathy with others. One child we cared for became horrified when she discovered for herself that "sloppy Joe" is, in her words, "mashed up cow."

To develop empathy is crucially important. In the early years of life, children in a caring and loving relationship with parents, develop the two faculties of empathy and self-control. It is empathy that enables us to feel as others feel, to walk in their shoes, and so to exercise kindness and consideration to others. We learn not to harm others because we know what that harm would feel like if it happened to us. This empathic faculty is the basis for the Golden Rule: do to others what you would have them do to you. Or, don't do to others that which you would not have them do to you. In either its positive or negative iteration the Golden Rule is found is all the world's great cultures, religions, and philosophical traditions. Scholars, like eighteenth century British philosopher David Hume, argued that empathy, the ability to feel sympathy for others, was the basis of human, hence moral, life. Contemporary brain science is adding scientific weight to the idea. (See, e.g., Rifkin's *The Empathic Civilization*, and Pinker's *The Better Angels of Our Nature*.)

Self-control is the faculty that helps us to restrain our worst urges. A great part of the parental task in the early years is to help children develop empathy and learn self-control. Those children who do not develop these faculties enter adult life troubled, and likely as not will cause trouble to others.

We have noticed time and again, that for many children entering foster care, these two faculties have not been developed. Abused children often do not have the ability to feel with others, nor the ability to control themselves. The absence of these skills accounts for much of the trouble children face in school and in the home. Our task is to re-parent children to help them to develop that which is missing.

For us, creating a nonviolent home, with its twin ideas of respect for others and control of the self, is at the heart of foster caring. As the production of meat, at least the way most meat is produced in developed economies like the United States, necessitates great cruelty to animals, we choose to be vegetarian. It is a lifestyle consistent with nonviolentism.

So enamored of meat is our culture that on occasion some have suggested to us that in not having meat in our home we deprive the children of some good. When Jane teaches new foster carers how to welcome children, she will suggest that foster carers find food that the children are familiar with. It provides comfort, and sameness, and an element of security. That makes sense. We have found that there is usually some nonmeat food that fits the bill. In some cases we take children to a burger place, to provide the necessary familiarity. But, any leftover meat does not come back to the house.

* * *

Nathan was a particularly difficult boy. He came to us at thirteen and had already suffered much. In the home he was surly, disrespectful, violent toward his siblings, and defiant. During the year he was with us he often mocked our vegetarianism. Driving down the road, he would laugh at "road kill," and would say, "If my dad was here, we'd have stopped and taken that baby home for supper." Nathan left us in difficult circumstances and went to live with other foster carers. When children leave, we are often left wondering how things worked out. We hope that we have done some good, but often we don't hear anything. We were surprised, some months later, during a conversation with his new foster dad at a support group meeting.

"Nathan's doing great!" said the amiable David. "Do you know what he said to us the other day? He starts telling us how important it is to be vegetarian. Gives me this whole speech about animal cruelty in factory farms. I could hardly believe my ears!"

* * *

Juanita is a grown woman now, and doing well attending college on the west coast. When she came to us, she was a troubled mid-teen passing through a "rebellious" stage. Part of her rebellion was tattoos, piercings, and experimenting with drugs. The drug abuse was the immediate reason she was in care. Her mom could not keep her safe. Part of her rebellion was, also, to become vegetarian. Juanita was a deeply sensitive and empathic young woman. Her vegetarianism was heartfelt. She breathed a sigh of relief when she discovered we were a vegetarian household. She actually cried. In her last foster home, she was forced to eat meat. Her carers there thought she was just being difficult. We cast no blame. When our eldest son became a vegetarian at age seven, for several years we misguidedly told him he had to eat at least some meat or fish for protein. We were simply ignorant of the facts of nutrition and healthy eating. Thankfully, in time we realized the sincerity of our son's conviction, educated ourselves about meat, and followed his lead.

We are not saying that all foster carers need to become vegetarian in their diet. We are sharing our own journey of nonviolentism and its implications for the way we view all sentient beings. That, for us, of necessity includes those beings that we choose to eat or not, and the story we tell about that to the children for whom we care.

11

Second-Hand Shock Syndrome and Caring for Yourself

In our culture we have gradually become used to hearing about PTSD. When a person is exposed to a direct trauma the psychological effects can be deep, long lasting, and profoundly disturbing. This diagnosis was first given to soldiers and those who were victims of war. Over time, it became a diagnosis given to those who suffer any direct trauma. We have cared for children and teenagers who have been diagnosed as suffering PTSD. Until recently, we had not understood that those who routinely care for the victims of trauma might suffer too. Ellie Izzo and Vicki Carpel Miller (2010) coined the phrase "Second-Hand Shock Syndrome" to account for this very real malady. They say:

> We believe that Second-Hand Shock Syndrome is a spectrum disorder that encompasses a wide range of physical, emotional, cognitive and spiritual effects from the indirect experience of trauma much like being in the presence of a smoker creates second-hand smoke. Over time, this can indirectly create disease in its recipient. The effects of trauma are contagious, adversely affecting your body, mind and spirit. (Kindle Locations 141–144)

In other words, live in the same environment as the traumatized and you will imbibe their trauma. Like all those who work with victims of trauma, foster carers are often subject to this syndrome. They continue:

> When we are first indirectly exposed to trauma, our brain begins to paint a picture for us by the activation of mirror neurons in the visual cortex. We see the event as if it were happening to us. A series of bio-physiological events then occur which results in the spilling out of chemicals into our bloodstream and throughout our body. This ultimately concludes in the over-production of cortisol that

contributes to the onset of many serious physical illnesses. (Kindle Locations 148–151)

Izzo and Miller claim that Second-Hand Shock Syndrome is where the trauma did not happen directly to the person, but nevertheless the person is involved through what he hears or sees. As all children in care are traumatized directly (as we have seen in earlier chapters) those who care for them through the repeated hearing or seeing the effects of trauma fall victim to the syndrome.

Re-parents are often exposed daily to the behaviors and stories of the traumatized. A casual conversation can expose a trauma and the conversation can quickly turn to a heavy subject. Once heard, the mind constructs a picture of the trauma, which is not easily forgotten. Over time the effect is cumulative.

* * *

Jane was driving. The children accompanying her were all chattering happily, and commenting on things they were seeing.

A little voice piped up, "Look at that cute dog over there."

Amidst the "oohs" and "aahs" another little voice said sadly, "I used to have a dog like that, but my step-dad locked it in a cage and wouldn't let me and my mum give it any food or water." (More revelations ensued, but we spare the reader the details of the poor dog's terrible suffering.)

Jane swallowed a couple of times and tried to focus, inwardly horrified at the description of cruelty she had just heard. She pushed aside her own feelings to start a conversation to distract all the children, and the conversation soon changed to lighter happenings. As the children spoke of pleasant things, still in Jane's mind the picture of the poor animal's suffering lingered. As she writes this, it lingers still. Many such exposures over the years to multiple traumas—in this book we have barely scratched the surface of what we have heard and seen—present the re-parent with mental and emotional challenges.

* * *

Foster carers are not the only people affected by Second-Hand Shock Syndrome. Izzo and Miller call it an epidemic in contemporary society. More than at any time in human history people are exposed to trauma through the pervasiveness of media images and stories. Television, the

Internet, newspapers, and social media are all full of disaster stories—often reliving horrible scenes hour by hour. As a culture it's possible that we are all suffering to some degree from Second-Hand Shock Syndrome. But as a foster carer, it sometimes feels that you are bombarded with story after story of abuse and trauma in a most personal and intimate way. A heavy weight often presses down.

In order to analyze further, we will look a little more closely at the various elements of the syndrome. These elements have been grouped in a variety of different, although similar ways, sometimes they are even used interchangeably. However, we will follow Izzo and Miller who identify three dimensions of Second-Hand Shock: compassion fatigue, secondary traumatic stress, and vicarious trauma. The three play upon each other in a complex psychological dance that scholars are only just beginning to understand.

Compassion Fatigue

Compassion fatigue is often called burnout. Izzo and Miller define it as "a long-term exhaustion built up by caring for others." Early signs of compassion fatigue are apathy, feeling less compassionate and less interested in the work one does. It is easy to see how foster carers can suffer from compassion fatigue. Their lives are spent caring for others with few breaks. One of the difficulties foster carers face is finding childcare if they need a break. Like many foster carers, we have found that often children in our care overlap, so there is not a period between one child leaving us and another coming. As we have seen, children in foster care cannot be looked after by anyone, nor can they just go to a friend's house. Everyone has to be checked out in advance. Obviously this is a needed safety plan, but it does make it more difficult for foster carers to take a spontaneous break.

In our experience, many foster carers are also really bad at saying "no" when asked if they can take another child or sibling group. This is because they care for the children. They hear the sad stories and want to help, and who wouldn't? Part of the initial foster care training emphasizes that foster carers should say "no" if they feel the child would be a poor fit in their current family, or simply one too many, but it is hard to do when faced with a phone call about a child who needs a bed for that night. There is always a greater need than resources available.

So, it is important for foster carers to be aware of and recognize the early signs of compassion fatigue and to do something before it gets too extreme.

Secondary Traumatic Stress

Secondary traumatic stress is usually seen in first responders to a tragedy. Although one usually thinks in terms of authorities as first responders, that is not always so. A first responder is anyone who hears about a traumatic incident first. It could be a friend, a colleague, a family member or a random stranger. Again this is something that foster carers are susceptible to. Children sometimes arrive straight from an abusive situation. The bruises and cuts are visible. In these cases the person who has overseen the child's removal from their home may be the first responder, but not always so.

Minutes after the caseworker had left Annie, Jane helped the child remove her sweater as she was getting hot. Jane saw with horror the extensive bruising around the child's neck and arms. A quick call was made to the caseworker's mobile phone asking her to return to the home so she could document the abuse.

It is more usual that there are no obvious signs of abuse. Often the children are quiet and withdrawn for a few days. Then, when safety is assured, the children become more confident and disclose neglect and abuse. Although that sounds quite simplistic, the process of disclosure of abuse is actually very complex. It may not happen for many months, sometimes even years. Sometimes it is triggered by an event or a smell. Often the beginning of the disclosure is just a sentence or two that leaves the foster carer alert. This may be followed by other comments over the next few weeks slowly allowing a picture to emerge. Nevertheless, the foster carers are the first people to hear about it. Secondary traumatic stress has symptoms very similar to PTSD. It leaves people feeling disturbed, and in extreme cases an emotional wreck. It can lead to depression and insomnia.

Vicarious Trauma

Psychologists are just beginning to understand vicarious trauma. According to the Vicarious Trauma Institute:

> Vicarious Trauma is what happens to your neurological (or cognitive), physical, psychological, emotional and spiritual health when you listen to traumatic stories day after day or respond to traumatic situations while having to control your reaction.

> Every time we interact from a position of compassion, controlling our empathic response with clients, patients, friends, congregants, strangers or neighbors, we are putting ourselves at risk. (2013)

Vicarious trauma is not a result of one tragedy but the impact of hearing multiple trauma stories on a regular basis. It also occurs when there is personal contact with the recipient of the trauma. All professional helpers and caregivers suffer from it to one degree or another. Put very simply, it is caused because the caregiver has to remain calm and nonreactive on the outside while listening to the trauma stories. On the inside there are lots of neurological activities as the horror of the stories impact the listener.

We have on many occasions sat and listened to stories that have horrified us, yet to the children we remain calm. We cannot allow the immediacy of our feelings about the abuse, or situation they are describing, be shown. It would be inappropriate to suggest to a child that an abuser be relieved of a part of his anatomy, even if that is what we are thinking. (Yes, even nonviolentists occasionally think that!) So we usually offer platitudes and reassurance. "I am sorry that happened to you" or "You know none of that was your fault." Of course, no disclosure of abuse is taken lightly, and all are documented for necessary action to be taken by DSS. However, when talking with the children it is important that our response is calm and controlled. Izzo and Miller call it "controlled empathy."

Again what makes foster carers especially vulnerable to vicarious trauma is that there are very few breaks from the children we care for. We do not go home from the office or store at night. There is also the additional pressure of confidentiality. Confidentiality is absolutely necessary to protect the young strangers we care for and their birth families. Yet, it means that to a large extent we hold the information. Of course, any new allegations are reported to the caseworker but even this does not help alleviate the repeated stories of trauma.

* * *

Lesley was a pretty ten-year-old with some learning difficulties, so she functioned more like a four- or five-year-old. A close relative had abused her, although the extent of the abuse was not revealed until she had been in foster care for a few weeks. Lesley told the story of the abuse, and the details of the relative who was the abuser, on a daily basis. We knew she could not start to heal until she had come to terms with it, so we listened. Daily for months and months we heard the story of the abuse. We knew the names of the abuser. We knew the details of the abuse. We saw how scared she was. At the same time we had other children who told us snippets of their stories. It can be relentless as neglect, abuse, and unhappy memories pour from those we care for.

We know we are fortunate in that we have each other to talk to. We know many foster carers who are parenting as single people. We think they are amazing!

A question we often consider is whether the children for whom we care can also suffer from Second-Hand Shock Syndrome. As far as we are able we protect the children from hearing of others' traumas, yet the children often talk very openly to each other about the abuse they suffered.

When a new young person is joining the family the kids in situ will often ask, "Why is she coming into foster care?" Our stock answer is, "You wouldn't want us to tell anyone your story so we won't tell you anyone else's story." That usually suffices and stops the questions. However, within days, sometimes even hours, they always seem to know everything about each other. This is not necessarily a bad thing. We have seen teenagers offer incredible support to each other. Yet we are concerned about how hearing about others' traumas will affect them.

* * *

Sally ran in off the school bus and announced that Jaden (who she sat next to) had said that she should "hit [name of abuser] around the head with a baseball bat if he tried to hurt her again." We were concerned, apart from the obvious confidentiality issues, Jaden should not have to listen to stories of sexual and physical abuse. We talked to Sally and gently explained that the middle school bus was not the best place to talk about what had happened to her in the past. That should be reserved for counselors, teachers, nurses, caseworkers, foster carers, etc. Sally was amazed, "But he asked why I lived with you and you are always telling me I shouldn't tell lies" The dilemma of foster carers! However, it made us aware that Second-Hand Shock Syndrome can be very real for children (even without the media) and those in foster care are especially vulnerable.

Caring for Yourself

Paul had left us. The enchanting eight-year-old had moved to be closer to his extended family. It was a good move and we were happy for him, though before he left we were unaware just how big a gap he would leave in our lives.

We had cared for Paul during a physically and emotionally hard ten months that required almost twenty-four hour a day care. Paul had numerous mental and emotional needs and functioned several years younger than his chronological age. He had a habit of asking the same simple questions again and again—literally hundreds of times. He was fixated on time, even though time had little meaning for him. He knew he went to bed at eight o'clock. It didn't matter what the actual time was, just as long as he was told "it's eight o'clock." We soon learned that to say something like, "Paul, you can stay up until eight-thirty tonight to finish watching your movie," would send him into a panic—for bed time could only be at eight. This obsessiveness could be quite appealing, as Paul was quite "cute." Paul's other side was not appealing. He could quickly work himself into a major tantrum for the smallest reason. In his tantrums Paul turned violent and we both had a few bruises to show for our care. His violence could be quite unpredictable throwing whatever came to hand—shoes, pieces of fruit, knives and forks from the dinner table, toys. We were lucky that he did no major damage while with us, though on occasion one of his flying objects hit one of our little pugs. Needless to say, the little dog gave Paul a wide berth after that. In addition to his mental and emotional challenges, Paul had a genetic physical disability that had remained untreated in his birth home. It required careful monitoring, much remedial work, and Jane attended lots of doctor and hospital appointments. To compound the issues, Paul and his siblings had been victims of neglect and abuse that had been ongoing for many years before coming to the attention of DSS. Due to the severity of the abuse and extreme needs of the children they had all been placed separately.

For ten months our lives had revolved around Paul's needs, and daily we had heard tales of his former life, including the repeated telling of the abuse he had suffered. We had seen huge improvements, including his physical issues, and to a small degree with his violent outbursts.

Now he had gone and we were both shocked at the level of exhaustion we felt. We moved from constant care and vigilance to nothing in the space of a day. It was a massive vacuum. For some time we were energy-less, plagued with headaches, sore throats and flu-like symptoms. Caring for Paul, however rewarding, had taken its toll. We are not alone in experiencing the psychological and emotional aftermath of deeply caring.

In all likelihood, those of us who choose to care for children in the fostering system do so because we want to make a difference—because we do truly care. It takes a certain kind of person. Foster carers are often the type of person who puts others' needs before their own. In truth, this is a large part of all parenting. Good parents and re-parents are other-regarding.

The downside of other-regarding-ness is that such carers sometimes forget to care for themselves. We have seen it many times where foster carers put so much into their children, and so much is taken out of themselves, that before long they burnout. It is compounded for carers by the secondary stress we noted above. Yet, even without the secondary stress the simple act of caring for others takes enormous amounts of emotional, mental, physical, and spiritual resources.

If we are to avoid burnout, or even worse breakdown, it is necessary to find a strategy that works to replenish the energy reserves and provides a kindness to ourselves. From observation and experience, there is no one-size-fits-all strategy. Nonetheless, *some* strategy is necessary. We provide here a set of strategies that work for us (some we both employ, and some are particular to each of us). We have found these strategies to be sufficient for us, but they are not necessary for everyone. We say sufficient in the philosophical rather than popular sense. In other words, each carer needs to find a *sufficient strategy*—one particular to them—to meet the *necessary need* of self-care. In other words, our strategy works for us, will work for some others, but will likely not work for all carers. But we do stress: *some coping mechanism needs to be put in place.*

We are aware also that the strategies are dependent on the ages of the children we care for. Some of the things we do now, caring mostly for teenagers, would not have worked with a houseful of little ones.

Mindfulness and Meditation

Arising from the Buddhist tradition, mindfulness is now widely recognized to be enormously helpful in reducing stress and helping live a balanced and thriving life. In simple terms, mindfulness practice is to become aware in each moment of feelings, thoughts, bodily sensations, the surrounding world, and our relationship to others, to live in the present moment, and in it all to find nonjudgmental acceptance. Life can be spoiled when we live either ruminating over the past, its mistakes and regrets, or else in the future, thinking about "what ifs." The past is over, the future is not yet, the present is what we have to deal with. Consciously becoming aware in each moment, neither regretting the past nor longing for the future is a great stress reducer.

Clinical studies have shown that meditation affects the brain in profound ways. For example, Simpkins and Simpkins have written two helpful books on Zen meditation and yoga and their use in helping people reduce stress and find balance (2011, 2012). They conclude, "neuroscience has provided evidence for some of the ancient claims about meditation. Clearly, meditation does bring about measurable changes in the brain and nervous system, and these changes can be helpful to clients" (2012, 31–32). They say:

> Zen meditation points us to direct experience, beyond our conceptualizations. Concepts tend to delimit experience to an interpretation. In the open felt moment without thought, we become attuned to our deeper, ever-changing and evolving nature, and from that as the foundation, we can find a natural, healthy, balanced way. (Simpkins and Simpkins 2012, 59)

The goal is to become mindful in small practical ways: mindfully breathing, mindfully eating, mindfully speaking, mindfully walking. This means to become aware of each breath, each mouthful of food, each word, and each step. Such attention to the present has the effect of centering and calming. However, it does not happen all at once, but only through steady daily practice. In the seminars and workshops that he teaches on stress and meditation Andy calls this a "life practice." It is not a "microwave" solution—pop it in the oven and in two minutes a ready meal. The benefits of mindfulness practice are long term. Though you can experience immediate stress relief by mindful breathing, it is the long-term effect of practicing to focus on each breath, learning to breathe more deeply from the abdomen and not the chest, which provides preventative emotional and physical health over time.

The human body is equipped with a remarkable system called the "autonomic nervous system" (ANS). Autonomic comes from two Greek words *auto*—self, and *nomos*—rule. The ANS functions largely in the background, outside of a person's control or awareness. The ANS has sympathetic and parasympathetic control systems that function at the visceral, involuntary level. The sympathetic is often popularly termed the "fight-or-flight" response; the parasympathetic, the "feed and breed" response. These remarkable systems kick in to allow the human body to function optimally. When faced with danger or external stimuli the sympathetic function causes breath to shorten, the heart to beat faster, the release of adrenalin, and gets you ready to fight the intruder or run away. At the same time, the sympathetic has the effect of shutting down the parasympathetic. This is no time to be digesting food or to feel romantic! All energy is directed to getting you out of danger. The parasympathetic, on the other hand, is the normal resting response, allowing the body to recharge. A balanced life is lived between the sympathetic and the parasympathetic. Both are essential.

However, contemporary life has caused us to live more and more within the sympathetic response system. People no longer linger over dinner, allowing the body to do the good and healthy work of digestion. Instead, they choose fast food and eat it on the run. Life is fast paced, with little time to do all they want to do. Each day finishes with the worry that all has not been achieved. For "relaxation" people choose video games that keep them on edge as they fight off the bad guys, or else they watch movies full of adrenalin surges that keep them on the edge of their seats. It's sympathetic overload! Add to that the fact that many of the interactions with foster children produce a sympathetic response, the plight of carers is exacerbated.

Mindfulness is a strategy that returns you again and again to the parasympathetic response. Over time, as the system is retrained, breathing slows down, reactions change. The mindful re-parent becomes the calmer re-parent. This helps not only in reactions to the children we care for, but also in the health and well-being of the foster carer.

How to Practice

When and how does one start a mindfulness practice? The simple answer is right now, by becoming aware. What is your breathing like? Become aware of what your body feels like. Be aware of emotions you are feeling. Notice your thinking. Be present to the environment around you. That is mindfulness! During the day, whenever you remember, simply bring yourself back to the present. There is no special equipment to purchase, no mindfulness designer clothes to buy, and no fees to be paid! Mindfulness slows things down, gives you time, and brings you fully into the present—not dwelling on the past, not worrying about the future.

For those who can find time and space (and we know that for many foster carers this is a major issue) specific periods of meditation can help to move you toward mindfulness. Short periods of concentrated meditation (say five to twenty minutes) somehow make it easier to be mindful at other times. Meditation is a particular practice of mindfulness. It is not *better* mindfulness, but it is a practice in a special way, for a certain time, perhaps in a particular place to train yourself what it feels like to be mindful. It is the particular practice of meditation that prepares you for mindfulness in the whole of life.

For many years, Andy has begun all his philosophy classes with several minutes of meditation. In philosophy, it is known as the discipline of *somaesthetics*, or body consciousness. In the western world, philosophers have been notorious for ignoring (sometimes even despising) the body. Andy is one of a growing number of philosophers who have begun to suggest that philosophy is more than detached thinking, and is rather *embodied* thinking—the mind in the body. Because it is the mind–body connection, simply thinking about it will not suffice. Somatic practice—from the Greek word for body, *soma*—is necessary. Hence, students whether taking social and political philosophy, or war and terrorism, or the ethics of love learn to connect the mind and body in meditation. Begun as an experiment, meditation has become an integral and welcome aspect of doing philosophy in Andy's classes. Repeatedly on course evaluations students mention how helpful the few minutes of meditation are in calming, centering, and preparing the students to engage in the activity of philosophy. Being still for a few minutes makes the rest of the class extra special. Andy teaches each course three times a week. If students attend every class, over a semester they will engage in forty-five sessions of meditation. If students take two classes in one semester with Andy, they engage in ninety meditation sessions. Even those students who are new to, or nervous about, meditation soon find they can very quickly "get in the zone."

How would that translate into the busy life of foster carers? At the beginning of Andy's classes students simply breathe for twenty cycles of Andy's breathing. He meditates at four or five breaths a minute, so the meditation takes about five minutes. At some point in any day, every one of us can find five minutes—even if it is just a trip to the bathroom! To find five minutes several times during a week will make a difference, as it does for Andy's students.

What happens during a meditation session? Nothing at all! And yet a great deal! In broad terms, there are two types of meditation: the *kataphatic* and the *apophatic*. The kataphatic is centered on images or words. This is the kind of meditation, often, where the meditation leader guides the group through a series of images or imaginations. The images are often pleasant or calming. (Though Jane, who has a fear of elevators, was once in such a meditation session when the leader suggested that the participants imagine themselves inside an elevator, ascending high. Whatever calming effect the meditation had had up to that point was lost in the total panic of being stuck in an elevator with no escape!)

The apophatic is wordless and imageless meditation—in its Zen version known as *zazen*—where the participant simply sits and is mindful of the breath. The meditator does not try to think of anything, nor not think of anything. She simply breathes and is aware. Thoughts are not played with or entertained, simply observed. This is the kind of meditation Andy teaches students at the beginning of his classes. It is a very simple and effective way into mindfulness practice. When the practitioner knows what mindfulness feels like in a meditation session, she knows how to return to it during everyday life—driving the car, washing the dishes, changing a diaper, sitting in a committee meeting, or standing in the checkout line.

Getting in Touch with Your Body

Here are our particular strategies to care for ourselves.

We are privileged to have a hot tub. It is an integral part of our deck, accessed through patio doors from the kitchen. For the last eight years, come rain or shine, warm weather or below freezing temperatures, the first thing we do early each morning, and very occasionally last thing before bed, is spend twenty minutes or so in the hot tub. We sit, we relax, we talk about the day to come, or the day just passed, we plan, we talk over the various doings of our foster children, feet are massaged, backs are rubbed, and aches and pains dissolve into the warm bubbly water. It is a way we care for ourselves. It is an oasis in often too busy days. But we have to sneak up early before the children wake!

Physical activity is so important—for all the mind–body connectedness reasons above, but also for health and general well-being. Jane's preferred exercise is Zumba—aerobic dance originally to Latin beat, but now much broader. Four or five times each week she is found with the other Zumba folk at the YMCA. It's good cardiovascular exercise, it's fun and challenging, it takes her mind off everything else, and it keeps her sane!

Andy's exercise for many years was the game of squash (like racquet ball played on an indoor court, but with different shaped racquets and a smaller less bouncy ball, and different rules). He still plays occasionally with colleagues at the university, but his preferred exercise is now *taijiquan* and *qigong*. Taiji (sometimes written t'ai chi) is a complete Chinese exercise system that includes mostly slow movements, performed in a routine, and is rooted in the ancient Chinese exercise system of qigong (energy work) and martial arts. It's the exercise TV documentaries show of massed ranks of older Chinese folk doing taiji in the park before their morning work. Though it looks easy, taiji is in fact extremely complex and takes a lifetime to master. Taiji people are called "players" and Andy plays taiji for at least an hour each day. (He is also a certified taiji instructor and holds a couple of classes most weeks).

Jane's almost daily Zumba, and Andy's daily taiji are ways we have found to care for ourselves, to recharge the energy batteries, to better help us care for our foster children.

Where do we find the time? In very busy schedules, we have found we have to make the time. We prioritize those things most important to us, and let other things go. Andy plays taiji in the early morning before work. Jane goes to Zumba in the early evenings after work. During those times we "tag-team" our care of our children and do household chores, supporting each other as we do that which is necessary to care for ourselves. This is more challenging for single carers, when there is no one to "tag-team" with. For Jane, as her Zumba is at the YMCA, it is possible for children to engage in other activities at the same time. The younger children can use the "Play and Stay" childcare facility, while the older ones enjoy playing basketball, table tennis, pool or swimming. Perhaps, such an arrangement would work for a single carer as many gyms include childcare arrangements.

An important element of self-care for foster carers is to use the system of respite care. In our county, carers who are willing to take another's children for an evening, or a weekend or even a week or two, place their names on a list that is distributed to all foster carers. We have found it helpful to make sure that every now and then we make some time for ourselves. Of course, we return the favor for other carers when they too need a break. Even so, respite care is often hard to find.

We have found these strategies to be helpful in caring for ourselves, and we offer them as examples only. Other carers, no doubt, will find different strategies. What is clear to us, though, is that whatever carers put in place, it is necessary to do so to avoid "crash and burn" scenarios.

Coming Face to Face with Your Own Violence

Caring for yourself is necessary, not only for general well-being as foster carers, but also because in the nature of the task you are brought time and again to face within yourself aspects of your psyche you find uncomfortable.

Jane has found, in training new foster carers and adopters, that a common response to hearing stories of abuse and violence against children for the first time is a horrified, "How could they possibly do that! They ought to be punished! They are inhuman!" One of the myths about violence that philosopher Barry Gan highlights in his book *Violence and Nonviolence* is the Myth of the Good Guys and Bad Guys. We have grown used to the myth of "us and them." "We," of course, are the good guys! The problem with the myth is that it oversimplifies the complexities of life. Not long after September 11, 2001, President Bush said, "You are either for us or against us." It became a bumper sticker in those emotionally fraught days after the terrorist atrocity. In a State of the Union speech he said also, "We must draw a line in the sand between us and the evil ones," and used the term, "the Axis of Evil" to speak of those perceived enemies of the United States. But, it was simplistic. It always is when we categorize people in such ways.

It is the case, too, when those of us involved in foster care see the child's abusers as "evil" and ourselves as paragons of virtue. Something much more nuanced is called for. There is great potential for violence in all of us. Becoming a nonviolentist is not merely voicing an opposition to violent actions in solving problems. It is rather an intentional commitment to oppose violence and to seek loving peaceful solutions that lead to human and nonhuman thriving.

Part of that intent is to take a look on the inside and face our own demons, our own potentiality to hurt others, to know the triggers that threaten to push us over the edge. In twelve-step programs the fourth step is to make a "searching and fearless moral inventory of ourselves" (Alcoholics Anonymous, 2013). Such a fearless taking stock is essential for any who take the path of caring for maltreated children. For the truth is, however calm and measured you may be most of the time, some of the behaviors you face from damaged children push you to the extreme. Though we have never hit a foster child, there have been occasions for both of us, when at our wit's end and completely out of inner resources, we have been tempted to hurt. Through long practice we are confident that we would never actually hit a child. However, on rare occasions we have given in to temptation to hurt and have used words that we knew in the using would cause pain to the child (even if the words were true!). We have always regretted it after the fact, and when possible have apologized to the child.

Such happenings reveal two things that are ultimately helpful. First, it shows us that we still have much "inner work" to do. This is the work you do through being utterly honest with yourself, your feelings, your potentiality to hurt others. It is the work you do through inner transformation using the techniques of mindfulness and meditation. The inner change occurs through habituation. We are what we most often do. Building the loving habits of nonviolence that we considered in chapter ten are transformative. At the end of the day, it is this habituation of nonviolence that has saved us from adding to the hurt others have already caused children in our care.

Second, it gives us empathy for those parents and caregivers who have physically hurt their children. Perhaps, after all, they are not "monsters" or inhuman. Perhaps, at the end of the day they are, as we all are, simply flawed people who have been pushed too far, and so out of their depth to hurt others was all that was left. With no role models in nonviolence, little family support, very little money, and sometimes fighting addiction, we can, at least, understand why some parents hurt their children.

12

Praxis: Creating a Nonviolent Home with the Ordinariness of Love

In this book we have told a part of our story of foster caring, and added our reflections on what we have come to call "loving nonviolent re-parenting." The children we have welcomed into our home as strangers have been victims of violence in multiple forms: physical, sexual, psychological, and systemic—each form of violence adding a further layer of hurt, fear, and rejection to fragile psyches. How are we to care for these tragic victims? What type of people are needed to fulfill the task? We have tried to answer these questions.

We coined the term re-parent. Children who have been parented in neglectful and violent ways need to be re-parented with loving care and nonviolence. The child victim of violence needs to experience a different way of relating to herself, to the adults in her life, to other children, and to nonhuman animals. If foster care as a system, or through individual carers, brings further violence into a child's life, we fail the child, and only reinforce old habits and patterns. At the end of the day much of the re-parenting task is mundane: to create a loving nonviolent home where children who have faced violence may feel safe, have their basic physical and psychological needs met, and grow into empathic, self-directed, decent people.

In part the book has been the telling of stories, and in part theoretical reflection on practice (what some philosophers have called *praxis*). We wanted the book to be more than theoretical and accessible to as many readers as possible. We have told stories to root our theory in the reality of daily care for children. The stories accomplish two things: first, we try to show the reader what it looks and feels like to care for children who have known violence; and second, we try to demonstrate what loving nonviolent care looks like in practice.

Stories are in themselves powerful. Without exception, the many kind readers who looked over our manuscript in different stages of completion were moved by the stories we have told. "I don't know how you can do that!" "I couldn't face what happened to those kids!" "I'd get too attached. I couldn't see them go back to a home where they were neglected!" "I wouldn't be able to work in a system where the system itself too often hurts and fails children!" "I couldn't let a kid do to my home what happened to yours!" "I had no idea!"

Stories are part of consciousness raising—helping people to see things unknown to them, or hidden from view. We hope that the stories we have told, even though a fraction of the incidents in our home over the last thirty plus years, help readers come to new awareness of the plight of half a million children in the United States. We hope we have raised awareness, too, of the great and pressing need for loving nonviolent carers to lend a hand, to be part of children's lives for at least a short time.

But consciousness raising is only part of the task of this book. In chapter seven, we considered the threefold process that applies to any kind of social change, any kind of progress: conscientization, internalization, and intentionalization. Having become aware, we need to do the hard and serious work of thinking through, working out, getting our heads around the issues and the possible solutions. We make the issues our own as we internalize disturbing realities and hopeful strategies. But even that is not enough. We need to act—to become part of something bigger than ourselves, something worthwhile, something noble, something that will make a difference.

We have included theoretical reflections to lay a good foundation for practice. Practices built on a shaky foundation will likely falter and prove ineffective. If we are to care for children who have been victims of violence, then we need to think deeply about that violence. For that reason we make no apologies for looking carefully at what violence is and how violence has affected children in care. We have looked too at why in our culture we have increasingly seen violence as wrong—morally and strategically.

To help us to do the difficult task of thinking about childhood victims of violence we turned for help to the ancient philosophers who asked the question: "How, then, shall we live?" their almost universal answer was not about keeping rules, or even about techniques to employ, but rather about the kinds of people we ought to be. What are the character traits of a good and wise person, someone who knows the secret of a life well-lived? So, as much as we have talked about children and their needs, we have looked at the carers themselves. We have considered the habits of loving nonviolence that produce the character traits of loving nonviolence. One who has become a loving nonviolent person is best suited for the task of caring for childhood victims of violence.

Being a foster carer has its costs and benefits. The reader will already have counted some of the costs with us as we have shared our story. We have written little about the financial costs of foster care, but not because it is unimportant. There is a clear financial cost, which is often misunderstood. We have, therefore, devoted an addendum to money issues. As we have shown in some of the stories, often children in care do not value the property of others. Carers soon learn to sit more loosely with their "stuff." If you hold on too tight, or too sentimentally, such is the road to heartache when a treasured object is broken or stolen. In chapter eleven we considered the mental and emotional costs, sometimes in quick bursts, often cumulative over time. These can be considerable, which is why we have devoted much thought to caring for ourselves in the midst of the mental and emotionally bruising times.

So why would anyone willingly choose to care for children who have been victims of family and systemic violence? The ancients told us that "virtue is its own reward," and we are tempted to say, without wanting to sound trite, that caring for our children has been reward enough. Social scientists have for some time noted that European and American culture has shifted from being largely "other-regarding" to "self-regarding." The literature is complex and there is by no means unanimity about either the diagnosis or prognosis for society. Whatever the truth, those who intentionally choose to care for the damaged children of others play their part in rebalancing the scales of "other-regardingness." It is not merely altruistic. We have sensed great joy when we hear of how well some of our children have done. We are proud when we hear of successful adults caring for their own children. We write this during graduation season. One of our boys posted wonderful photos on Facebook as he graduated from the local community college with excellent grades. He is a musician and as soon as we finish this paragraph we'll be taking off to our town's summer festival. Our former foster child will be performing live on stage. Reward enough!

* * *

The snow was gently falling—large flakes, drifting almost weightlessly covering every twig with frosting. This was the first snowfall of what would be a long winter. We had 105 inches in the three months January to March. We lazed in the hot tub, the warmth of water on bodies juxtaposed with the tingling pin-pricks of snow on shoulders and faces. Such times are magic. We often daydream in our morning soak. We will be retiring from foster care soon, and on this day our daydreams turned to foster care.

"So, in a more perfect world," Andy said, brushing snow from the rim of his glasses, "What would you like to see in foster care?"

"You mean if I could have three wishes for those who will become carers after our time?" Jane responded.

"Yes, if you like. Or we could make it more specific, what three things would you like our book to accomplish?"

We chatted for a while, then fell in with the silence of the morning. After a while we gathered our thoughts.

"I suppose, I would love to see 'loving nonviolent re-parenting' to be taken seriously by agencies, carers, and those who have responsibility for setting policies," Jane reflected. "More so than now, anyway."

"Yes, I suspect that even in the agencies we have worked with not everyone is on board with intentional nonviolence," Andy said. "Some folk like to hold on to the notion that violence as a last resort tends to work. Kids need a good spanking if you've tried everything else, they say."

"But, it's so counterproductive with the population of children we've worked with," Jane replied, a little sadly. "Education, training courses, workshops, giving intentional nonviolence a higher priority would be great. I hope our book nudges things that way."

"And what would your second wish be?" Andy said with a smile.

"I see a dearth of experienced foster carers. I wish that foster care was taken more seriously—professionally seriously I mean. Since the Clinton Act, foster carers are pushed to adopt the children placed in their homes. Once a house is full, those newly trained foster carers who have become adopters are lost to the system. It means that carers no longer have the option of becoming more skilled over time with the kinds of difficult behaviors we have seen again and again. It takes time and many placements to develop the skills needed. We no longer have a pool of truly experienced foster carers to draw on."

"I agree," Andy replied. "I'd even suggest that foster care should be a career. Probably on a par with caseworkers in terms of a salary . . . "

"A base salary for being a foster carer, then a boarding allowance for each child in your home," Jane interrupted animatedly. "You'd feel more part of a professional team. You'd have more time to work with other supporting agencies, instead of panicked phone calls after work when it's nearly impossible to get through to the people you need to. I'd have loved that."

"I've had two wishes," Jane said. "You can have the third. What would you wish for?"

"I think my wish is more pragmatic. So often I've seen carers deeply hurt, feeling like a failure when they have not seen progress with their children, or when the child reverts to former ways. My wish is that our book would give a realistic expectation of the possibilities of care. We do our best, but some children are so deeply damaged by the time they come to into foster care that we can do little. It's not their fault. It's not our fault. Sometimes it's not even the fault of their birth parents."

"Yes, realistic expectations. I like that," Jane replied reflectively. "We might not always get it right. We might not be able to 'fix' the kids in our care."

"But we bring a bit of love . . ."

"And stability . . ."

"And safety . . ."

"And freedom from violence . . ."

"At least for a time . . ."

We fell silent with the snow again.

* * *

As a family we like to celebrate. New Year's Eve for us is one such celebration each year when we invite family and friends to enjoy food and drink and "see in the New Year." More or less every December 31, for as long as we can remember, we have a house full. Depending on our guests, music can play a large part.

On this particular night we had a full band: three guitarists, a bass player, a hand drummer, a ukulele player, and Rufus, our twelve-year-old harmonica playing child. Rufus had not had an easy life with family disruption, uncertainty, and eventual foster care. By accident one day we discovered he had a natural affinity with the blues harp. Seemingly from nowhere he knew how to bend notes, harmonize, and somehow fit in with an ensemble. Andy (being a musician himself) encouraged Rufus, and for Christmas we bought him a set of harps in twelve different keys. This night, with his little porkpie hat perched jauntily at an angle and his box of harps, Rufus had a wonderful time. As long as the leader of any particular song shouted out the key, Rufus would produce the harp in the correct key and play along. In many respects it was a very ordinary time. It is what good families and friends do when they gather to celebrate life. In other respects it was a magical time. For his year or so with us, Rufus experienced loving nonviolent care after too many incidences of violence. In our mind's eye, we see Rufus as he was on that New Year's Eve, full of life, full of swagger, utterly safe, and unafraid. Such is love.

Addendum

Money Can't Buy Me Love

People make many assumptions about money and foster care. Many of the assumptions are simply wrong, or misguided. In this addendum we want to take an honest look at finances. It's the elephant in the room. Do foster carers only do it for the money? Some do, most do not. To do foster care well you cannot do it for the money. Shouldn't foster carers do the job simply for love of children? Absolutely not! To do so would be like asking school teachers to teach for the love of it, or veterinarians to do their work for the love of animals. But just how does the money thing work in foster care? Of all the issues, this is perhaps the closest to a taboo—something not to be spoken of. It is also the area where foster carers often face difficulties.

Every child who comes into care is given a boarding allowance. With all the authorities we have fostered for, the allowance comes in two parts: a general allowance and a clothing allowance. According to the New York State Office of Children's and Family Services, maximum foster care subsidies range from $17.48 to $23.84 per day, depending on the age of the child (2013). "Special" children are rated at $38.33 a day, with "exceptional" children at $58.10. To have children placed as "special" requires mental health documentation, developmental delay, probation, and such things. Exceptional children require twenty-four hours a day care. Foster carers usually receive all children on the basic rate, and must file a form containing documents with evidence why the child's rate should be higher. Factors include that the child is a JD/PINS, or a mental health diagnosis, or the child is on certain psychiatric drugs to be administered by the foster carer. The figures we quote are maximum rates, and rates vary between counties in New York.

The allowance is paid in arrears. If a child arrives on, say the sixth of the month, the allowance will be paid for the current month on the fifteenth of the following month. In other words, the foster carer will receive payment for the sixth to the thirtieth in the middle of the following month. If a sibling group of say, three children, arrives early in the month, the foster carers will need to provide for the children for up to six weeks without receiving any allowance from DSS. For that reason, in initial training and vetting, it is said that foster carers must have jobs that will adequately pay normal household bills and living expenses. Foster care cannot be considered as the only paying job for a family.

How much does it cost to care for children? According to the United States Department of Agriculture in 2012 the average American family spend $241,080 to raise a child from birth to age eighteen (USDA 2013). Clearly, children require different costs at different ages, and by and large we can assume that as children get older they cost more money. The report says, "For the year 2012, annual child-rearing expenses per child for a middle-income, two-parent family ranged from $12,600 to $14,700, depending on the age of the child." It amounts to $36.69 a day, averaged out over eighteen years, and gives us a base line for looking at the costs of raising a child. How does this figure compare with foster care basic boarding allowance we cited above? Poorly. Based on government figures, then, what foster carers receive as an allowance is far below the average cost of caring for a child. In other words, it is barely adequate. The United States government, recognizing this fact, does not consider the foster care boarding allowance as income for tax purposes, and rightly so.

The boarding allowance covers the child's ordinary and basic needs. But troubled children do not always behave "normally." In foster caring we had to get used to children being suspended from school with some regularity. What happens when a child receives out of school suspension for a few days? The foster carers have to find some way for the child to be cared for during school hours. Schools in our area used to have in school suspension for minor infractions. When the economic squeeze came the schools could no longer afford teachers to cover in school suspension, so children receive out of school suspension for the same issues.

We leave the house for work at 7:30 (Jane) and 9:00 (Andy). Jane returns at 3:00 and Andy at 5:30–6:00 (on an average day). This means finding some form of childcare for at least six hours. According to a survey carried out by the New York State Office of Children's and Family Services, in 2014–2015 the average childcare rate was $10.00 an hour (2014). A child suspended from school would require at least six hours care a day, or $60.00. If the foster carers receive, say $23.00 boarding allowance, then more than two days allowance would be needed merely to provide for childcare for one day. This would be on top of the child's ordinary ongoing daily costs.

Another solution is for the foster carers to take a day's leave from work. For us, though we are salaried (we work a ten-month-year in education) if we take our average hourly rate based on a thirty-five hour week over 52 weeks, it would be over $39.00 an hour. For one of us to take a day's leave would be effectively $273.00 each day for a child's suspension. It does not require a math genius to see quickly how these unseen costs mount up. Even so, to take a day's leave is not always possible. During semester time we cannot simply take days off work. Conversely, in the summer months when we are not under contract the situation eases. Those who don't work in education will face similar difficulties.

What are the other unseen costs of foster care?

* * *

Jane heard an enormous bang. She rushed upstairs hoping no one had been hurt. As she reached the top of the stairs the laughter reached her.

"What was that bang?"

Apparently one of the boys we were caring for had decided to hold a door shut on one of the girl's bedrooms to prevent her leaving. The girl had pushed back very hard on one of the door's wooden panels. It had shattered.

There was no malice, it was just "good fun," and both children were laughing about it. However, the fractured door panel and a damaged handle required a new door. To make matters worse, in our old house, the door was not a standard size.

* * *

There is more than the average wear and tear on the house. As a general rule of thumb, we have learned that foster children do not take the same care of our property as we do. There are many nonaccidental breakages. There is much greater need of redecoration. Upkeep costs increase substantially.

Losses can't always be measured in monetary terms—some things are irreplaceable.

* * *

Jumon was angry—very angry. It was more than the irritation of being reminded that his room needed to be tidied. One of the most pleasant and easy young teenagers we have cared for, Jumon had learned the day before that his mother, who had been successfully in rehab, had returned to drink. Jumon had been hoping to be reunited with her soon. His hopes were dashed. Being reminded of his untidy room was just the last straw.

When his anger peaked he was in the middle of eating a large bowl of breakfast cereal, with at least a half pint of milk still in the large bowl. In a fit of rage he hurled the bowl at the kitchen shelves. The bowl shattered and the milk saturated the contents of the shelf. It happened that this was the shelf with our photo albums containing the photos of our children from birth until the digital revolution in the late 1990s. The albums were soaked. Milk seeped into the plastic covering the photos. We did our best to clean it up, but much spilled milk remained. After a day or two the albums began to smell of stale milk. It was only some months later when we went to show friends some early pictures that we realized that many of the most precious photos were ruined. Milk reacts with Kodak photo paper in a bad way.

In monetary terms, these old photos were worth very little. In terms of memory and sentiment, these photos were irreplaceable. Their loss was a different kind of hidden cost. But, as they say, "No use crying over spilt milk!"

* * *

Text message conversation between Andy and Jane:
Andy: I've got the solution.
Jane: To what?
Andy: The car issue. We trade the car and get a minivan
Jane: What? U said u would never have one
Andy: I know. It's a moment of weakness. I just give in. I've called the dealer. Going down later.

Two days later we were the proud owners of an eight-seat Honda Odyssey minivan. To be honest, not really proud, for Andy in middle age did not see himself as a minivan driver! But it had become a necessity. We were tired of every local journey needing two cars and both of us to drive. And now we had a vacation planned. We wanted to be able to talk together and share the seven-plus hour drive. Where else can you put five children when you are going camping at the ocean?

These cars do not come cheap. Nor are they cheap to run. It is another hidden cost of foster care.

When you have the car large enough to transport the whole family, you plan a road trip. Our grown sons live fifteen and twenty-four hours away by car. Stops on route are a necessity—at least one night each way. With multiple foster children it requires at least two motel rooms, sometimes three depending on the gender of the children. That doubles or triples the cost. When you get to the destination, the chances are that the folk you are going to see do not have room to accommodate you and all the kids. More motel rooms needed, or hiring a house large enough through something like Vacation Rentals By Owners—a great resource, but you can watch your bank balance go down pretty fast! As an example, one fall break we decided to take a week's vacation in North Carolina. At the time we had a sixteen-year-old girl and nine- and eleven-year-old brothers. We had hired a three-bedroomed house near the beach. Even out of season this house cost $850. Then the trip took two days driving each way, with a stop overnight at a roadside motel. We needed three rooms, at around $65 each. And then there are meals out. There is a vast difference in the bill between just the two of us, and the two of us plus three to five children. It is easy to see how quickly costs escalate.

When we were fostering in the United Kingdom the policy was to take the annual boarding allowance and divide it into fifty-six weeks rather than fifty-two. One extra week was paid just before Christmas, one extra week just before the child's birthday, and two weeks just before the long summer break from school. This proved very useful in having extra cash to make Christmas, birthdays, and vacations memorable for the children.

In New York, there is no extra help for Christmas, birthdays, and vacations. These special events are seen just as a part of normal family life. But they run expensive!

* * *

"Andy, I just had a call from DSS. Can we take an extra boy? It won't be a long placement. He had returned home, but it hasn't worked out. He's planning to sign himself out of care on his eighteenth birthday."

"Why not!" Andy replied to Jane, "One more can't make a difference. And besides, it's Christmas!"

We already had three other teens, all much the same age as Robbie. He arrived a couple of hours later and all the children proudly showed him the newly decorated Christmas trees.

"What are we going to get Robbie for Christmas?" Jane asked Andy that night.

We already had iPods with names engraved on them hidden away for the two girls, and a handheld games machine for Daiquan.

"Well, we can't get Robbie anything less. That would feel awful for him. Let's get him the same as Daiquan in a different color."

At the time, these machines were around $200 each, plus games to play on them. We have a tradition of making up stockings with goodies in them for the children. Robbie got a stocking too. This was not going to be a cheap Christmas!

Two weeks after Christmas Robbie turned eighteen.

"Do you think we ought to celebrate Robbie's eighteenth? It's an important birthday, and we should at least acknowledge it," Andy had said a few days before.

Birthday presents were duly bought, given and received with thanks. We shared a meal to celebrate at a favorite restaurant. A couple of days later Robbie left us as he signed himself out of DSS care. He was grateful for the time spent with us, even though it was less than a month. In terms of money, Robbie had been a very expensive placement!

"Jane! Jane! Jane!" came the insistent voice across the local park where Jane was spending some time with a current child in our care.

Jane looked up to see a young man detach himself from a group of young people in their early twenties supervising toddlers in the play-ground, and run toward her.

"Robbie is that you? You look great!"

"That's my little one over there," Robbie replied pointing to a blonde haired toddler. "We're expecting another too!" he grinned, indicating his heavily pregnant girlfriend.

Robbie had been with us only three and a half weeks, yet bonds had been established. For Robbie his Christmas in foster care had been memorable.

It's not about the money!

Appendix

Definitions of Child Abuse, Maltreatment, and Neglect in New York

N.Y. SOS. LAW Child Abuse, Ma- Section 412:
When used in this title and unless the specific context indicates otherwise: 1. An "abused child" means: (a) a child under eighteen years of age not in "residential care," as defined in subdivision four of section four hundred twelve-a of this title, and who is defined as an abused child by the family court act; or (b) a child under the age of eighteen years who is defined as an abused child in residential care pursuant to subdivision one of section four hundred twelve-a of this title; 2. A "maltreated child" includes: (a) a child under eighteen years of age not in "residential care" as defined in subdivision four of section four hundred twelve-a of this title: (i) defined as a neglected child by the family court act, or (ii) who has had serious physical injury inflicted upon him or her by other than accidental means; or (b) a child who is a neglected child in residential care as defined in subdivision two of section four hundred twelve-a of this title; 3. "Person legally responsible" for a child means a person legally responsible as defined by the family court act; 4. "Subject of the report" means: (a) any parent of, guardian of, or other person eighteen years of age or older legally responsible for, as defined in subdivision (g) of section one thousand twelve of the family court act, a child reported to the statewide central register of child abuse and maltreatment who is allegedly responsible for causing injury, abuse or maltreatment to such child or who allegedly allows such injury, abuse or maltreatment to be inflicted on such child; or a director or an operator of, or employee or volunteer in, a home operated or supervised by an authorized agency, the office of children and family services, or an office of the department of mental hygiene or in a family day-care home, a day-care center, a group family day care

home, a school-age childcare program or a day-services program who is allegedly responsible for causing injury, abuse or maltreatment to a child who is reported to the statewide central register of child abuse or maltreatment or who allegedly allows such injury, abuse, or maltreatment to be inflicted on such child; or (b) a subject of a report of an abused or neglected child in residential care as defined in subdivision eight of section four hundred twelve-a of this title; 5. "Other persons named in the report" shall mean and be limited to the following persons who are named in a report of child abuse or maltreatment other than the subject of the report: (a) the child who is reported to the statewide central register of child abuse and maltreatment; and such child's parent, guardian, or other person legally responsible for the child who has not been named in the report as allegedly responsible for causing injury, abuse or maltreatment to the child or as allegedly allowing such injury, abuse or maltreatment to be inflicted on such child; or (b) other persons named in a report of an abused or neglected child in residential care as defined in subdivision nine of section four hundred twelve-a of this title; 6. An "unfounded report" means any report made pursuant to this title unless an investigation determines that some credible evidence of the alleged abuse or maltreatment exists; 7. An "indicated report" means a report made pursuant to this title if an investigation determines that some credible evidence of the alleged abuse or maltreatment exists. 8. "Substance abuse counselor" or "alcoholism counselor" means any person who has been issued a credential therefor by the office of alcoholism and substance abuse services, pursuant to paragraphs one and two of subdivision (d) of section 19.07 of the mental hygiene law. (Find Law for Legal Professionals n.d. a)

N.Y. FCT. LAW § 1012 : NY Code—Section 1012:
When used in this article and unless the specific context indicates otherwise: (a) "Respondent" includes any parent or other person legally responsible for a child's care who is alleged to have abused or neglected such child; (b) "Child" means any person or persons alleged to have been abused or neglected, whichever the case may be; (c) "A case involving abuse" means any proceeding under this article in which there are allegations that one or more of the children of, or the legal responsibility of, the respondent are abused children; (d) "Drug" means any substance defined as a controlled substance in section thirty-three hundred six of the public health law; (e) "Abused child" means a child less than eighteen years of age whose parent or

other person legally responsible for his care (i) inflicts or allows to be inflicted upon such child physical injury by other than accidental means which causes or creates a substantial risk of death, or serious or protracted disfigurement, or protracted impairment of physical or emotional health or protracted loss or impairment of the function of any bodily organ, or (ii) creates or allows to be created a substantial risk of physical injury to such child by other than accidental means which would be likely to cause death or serious or protracted disfigurement, or protracted impairment of physical or emotional health or protracted loss or impairment of the function of any bodily organ, or (iii) commits, or allows to be committed an offense against such child defined in article one hundred thirty of the penal law; allows, permits or encourages such child to engage in any act described in sections 230.25, 230.30 and 230.32 of the penal law; commits any of the acts described in sections 255.25, 255.26 and 255.27 of the penal law; or allows such child to engage in acts or conduct described in article two hundred sixty-three of the penal law provided, however, that (a) the corroboration requirements contained in the penal law and (b) the age requirement for the application of article two hundred sixty-three of such law shall not apply to proceedings under this article. (f) "Neglected child" means a child less than eighteen years of age (i) whose physical, mental or emotional condition has been impaired or is in imminent danger of becoming impaired as a result of the failure of his parent or other person legally responsible for his care to exercise a minimum degree of care (A) in supplying the child with adequate food, clothing, shelter, or education in accordance with the provisions of part one of article sixty-five of the education law, or medical, dental, optometrical or surgical care, though financially able to do so or offered financial or other reasonable means to do so; or (B) in providing the child with proper supervision or guardianship, by unreasonably inflicting or allowing to be inflicted harm, or a substantial risk thereof, including the infliction of excessive corporal punishment; or by misusing a drug or drugs; or by misusing alcoholic beverages to the extent that he loses self-control of his actions; or by any other acts of a similarly serious nature requiring the aid of the court; provided, however, that where the respondent is voluntarily and regularly participating in a rehabilitative program, evidence that the respondent has repeatedly misused a drug or drugs or alcoholic beverages to the extent that he loses self-control of his actions shall not establish that the child is a neglected child in the absence of evidence establishing that the child's physical, mental, or emotional condition has been impaired or is in imminent danger of becoming impaired as set forth in paragraph (i) of this subdivision; or (ii) who has been abandoned, in accordance with the definition and other criteria set forth in subdivision five of section three hundred eighty-four-b of the social services law, by his parents or other person legally responsible for his care. (g) "Person legally responsible" includes the child's custodian, guardian, any other person responsible for the child's care at the relevant time. Custodian may include any person continually or at regular intervals found in the same household as the child when the conduct of such person causes or contributes to the abuse or neglect of the child. (h) "Impairment of emotional health" and "impairment of mental or emotional condition" includes a state of substantially diminished psychological or intellectual functioning in relation to, but not limited to, such factors as failure to thrive, control of aggressive or self-destructive impulses, ability to think and reason, or acting out or misbehavior, including incorrigibility, ungovernability, or habitual truancy; provided, however, that such impairment must be clearly attributable to the unwillingness or inability of the respondent to exercise a minimum degree of care toward the child. (i) "Child pro-tective agency" means the child protective service of the appropriate local department of social services or such other agencies with whom the local department has arranged for the provision of child protective services under the local plan for child protective services or an Indian tribe that has entered into an agreement with the state department of social services pursuant to section thirty-nine of the social services law to provide child protective services. (j) "Aggravated circumstances" means where a child has been either severely or repeatedly abused, as defined in subdivision eight of section three hundred eighty-four-b of the social services law; or where a child has subsequently been found to be an abused child, as defined in paragraph (i) or (iii) of subdivision (e) of this section, within five years after return home following place-ment in foster care as a result of being found to be a neglected child, as defined in subdivision (f) of this section, provided that the respondent or respondents in each of the foregoing proceedings was the same; or where the court finds by clear and convincing evidence that the parent of a child in foster care has refused and has failed completely, over a period of at least six months from the date of removal, to engage in ser-vices necessary to eliminate the risk of abuse or neglect if returned to the parent, and has failed to secure services on his or her own or otherwise adequately prepare for the return home and, after being informed by the court that such an admission could eliminate the requirement that the local department of social services provide reunification services to the parent, the parent has stated in court under oath that he or she intends to continue to refuse such necessary services and is unwilling to secure such services independently or otherwise prepare for the child's return home; provided, however, that if the court finds that adequate justification exists for the failure to engage in or secure such services, including but not limited to a lack of childcare, a lack of transportation, and an inability to attend services that conflict with the parent's work schedule, such failure shall not constitute an aggravated circumstance; or where a court has determined a child five days old or younger was abandoned by a parent with an intent wholly to abandon such child and with the intent that the child be safe from physical injury and cared for in an appropriate manner. (k) "Permanency hearing" means a hearing held in accordance with section one thousand eighty-nine of this act for the purpose of reviewing the foster care status of the child and the appropriateness of the permanency plan developed by the social services district or agency. (Find Law for Legal Professionals n.d. b)

References

Ackerman, Peter, and Jack Duvall. 2000. *A Force More Powerful: A Century of Nonviolent Conflict.* New York: Palgrave.

American Academy of Child and Adolescent Psychiatry. March 2011. *Reactive Attachment Disorder.* Facts for Families No. 85. Accessed January 28, 2012. http:// www.aacap.org/cs/root/facts_for_families/reactive_attachment_disorder.

American College of Surgeons/Health Policy Research Institute. 2010. *The Surgical Workforce in the United States: Profile and Recent Trends.* Accessed May 14, 2015. http://www.acshpri.org/documents/ACSHPRI_Surgical_Workforce_in_US_apr2010.pdf.

American Psychological Association. "Violence in the Media—Psychologists Study TV and Video Game Violence for Potential Harmful Effects." Accessed May 19, 2014. http://www.apa.org/research/action/protect.aspx.

Anonymous, Alcoholics. 2013. *The Big Book of Alcoholics Anonymous.* Special Edition.

BAAF Adoption and Fostering. 2105. "Statistics England." Accessed May 7, 2015. http://www.baaf.org.uk/res/statengland. Benedict, Mary I. July 1994. "Types and Frequency of Child Maltreatment by Family Foster Care Providers in an Urban Population." *Child Abuse & Neglect* 18 (7): 577–85.

Bowlby, John. 1982. *Attachment and Loss Volume 1 Attachment.* New York: Basic Books.

———. 1973. *Attachment and Loss Volume II Separation: Anxiety and Anger.* New York: Basic Books.

———. 1980. *Attachment and Loss Volume III Loss Sadness and Depression.* New York: Basic Books.

Briere, John N. 1992. *Child Abuse Trauma: Theory and Treatment of the Lasting Effects.* Newbury Park: Sage.

Center for Development of Human Services (CDHS). 2014. *Leaders Guide. Group Preparation and Selection of Foster and/or Adoptive Familes II. Model Approaches to Partnership in Parenting (MAPP).* Buffalo.

Center for Disease Control and Prevention. 2014. *Adolescent and Teen Health.* Accessed June 9, 2014. http://www.cdc.gov/healthyyouth/Sexualbehaviors/ index.htm.

Center for Effective Discipline. 2014. *Discipline at School (NCACPS).* Canal Winchester, OH. http://www.stophitting.com/index.php?page=statesbanning.

Child Trends Data Bank (CTDB). 2013. *Attitudes Toward Spanking: Indicators on Children and Youth.*

———. 2014. *Indicator List for Teen Pregnancy/Reproductive Health*. Accessed May 28, 2015. http://www.childtrends.org/databank/indicators-by-topic-area/teen-pregnancyreproductive-health/.

———. *Child Maltreatment*. Accessed May 12, 2015. http://www.childtrends.org/?indicators=child-maltreatment.

Child Welfare Information Gateway. 2011. *Foster Care Statistics 2010*. Washington, DC. Accessed January 27, 2012. http://www.childwelfare.gov/pubs/factsheets/foster.cfm.

———. 2012a. *Concurrent Planning: What the Evidence Shows*. Washington, DC.

———. 2012b. *Adoption, Disruption, and Dissolution*. Washington, DC.

Childs-Gowell, Elaine. 2000. *Re-parenting Schizophrenia: The Cathexis Experiment*. Bloomington: iUniverse.

Delap, Emily, and Louise Melville. 2011. *Fostering Better Care: Improving Foster Care Provision around the World*. EveryChild.

Department for Children, Schools and Families. 2008. *Statistical First Release*. London. Accessed May 28, 2015. http://www.education.gov.uk/rsgateway/DB/SFR/s000810/SFR23_2008_Text_V1.pdf.

De Waal, Frans. 2009. *The Age of Empathy: Nature's Lessons for a Kinder Society*. New York: Three Rivers Press.

Douglas, Jack, Jr. 2012. "Foster Kids Abuse Case: 'Should We Be Embarrassed?'" *CBS News 11*. Accessed May 28, 2015. http://dfw.cbslocal.com/2012/05/16/foster-kids-abuse-case-we-should-be-embarrassed/.

Edwards, Susan M. 1989. *"Policing 'Domestic Violence' Women, the Law and The State."* London: Sage.

Find Law for Legal Professionals. n.d. a. *N.Y. SOS. LAW § 412: NY Code—Section 412: General Definitions*. Accessed May 31, 2015. http://codes.lp.findlaw.com/nycode/SOS/6/6/412.

———. n.d. b. *N.Y. FCT. LAW § 1012: NY Code—Section 1012: Definitions*. http://codes.lp.findlaw.com/nycode/FCT/10/1/1012.

Finkelhor, David. 1979. *Sexually Victimized Children*. New York: Free Press.

———. 1986. *A Sourcebook on Child Sexual Abuse*. Newbury Park: Sage.

Finkelhor, David, Richard J. Geles, Gerald T. Hotaling, and Murray A. Straus. 1983. *The Dark Side of Families: Current Family Violence Research*. Thousand Oaks, CA: Sage.

Finkelhor, David, and Lisa Jones. 2006. "Why have Child Maltreatment and Child Victimization Declined." *Journal of Social Issues* 62 (4): 685–716.

Fitz-Gibbon, Andrew. 2012. *Love as a Guide To Morals*. VIBS Ethical Theory and Practice Series. Amsterdam: Rodopi.

———. 2014. "The Ethics of Care and Violence." Michael Brown and Katy Gray Brown *Nonviolence: Critiquing Assumptions, Examining Frameworks*. Amsterdam: Rodopi.

Gan, Barry L. 2013. *Violence and Nonviolence: An Introduction*. Lanham: Rowman and Littlefield.

Gandhi, Mahatma. 1962. *The Essential Gandhi: An Anthology of His Writings on Life, Work, and Ideas*. Edited by Louis Fischer. New York: Vintage.

———. 2001. *Non-Violent Resistance (Satyagraha)*. Mineola, NY: Dover.

Gerbner, George, Catherine J. Ross, and Edward Zigler. 1980. *Child Abuse: An Agenda for Action*. Oxford: Oxford University Press.

Grossman, Dave. 1995. *On Killing: The Psychological Cost of Learning to Kill in War and Society*. New York: Back Bay Books.

———. Fall 2000. "Teaching Kids to Kill." *National Forum.* Phi Kappa Phi.

Grug, Etienne G., Linda L. Dahlberg, James A. Mercy, Anthony B. Zwi, and Rafael Lozano, eds. 2002. *World Report on Violence and Health.* Geneva: World Health Organization.

Hobbes, Georgina F., Christopher J. Hobbs, and Jane M. Wynne. December 1999. "Abuse of Children in Foster and Residential Care." Child Abuse & Neglect 23 (12): 1239–52.

Holmes, Robert L., and Barry L. Gan. 2011. *Nonviolence in Theory and Practice.* 3rd edition. First edition 1990. Long Grove: Waveland Press.

Hopper, Jim. 2012. *Child Abuse: Statistics, Research and Resources.* Accessed May 28, 2015. http://www.jimhopper.com/abstats/.

Izzo, Ellie, and Vicki Carpel Miller. 2010. *Second-Hand Shock: Surviving & Overcoming Vicarious Trauma.* Scottsdale, AZ: High Conflict Institute Press. Kindle Edition.

King, Jr., Martin Luther. 1986. *A Testament of Hope: The Essential Writings and Speeches of Martin Luther King Jr.* Edited by James M. Washington. San Francisco, CA: Harper.

Lyman, Bobby Jo, ed. December 2003. *Journal of Prenatal and Perinatal Psychology and Health.*

MacIntyre, Alasdair. 1967. *A Short History of Ethics: A History of Moral Philosophy from the Homeric Age to the Twentieth Century.* London: Routledge.

———. 1985. *After Virtue: A Study in Moral Theory.* London: Duckworth.

———. 1988. *Whose Justice? Which Rationality?* London: Duckworth.

———. 1990. *Three Rival Versions of Moral Inquiry: Encyclopaedia, Genealogy, and Tradition.* London: Duckworth.

———. 1999. *Dependent Rational Animals: Why Human Beings Need the Virtues.* Peru, IL: Open Court.

Marshall, Michael J. 2002. *Why Spanking Doesn't Work.* Springville, UT: Bonneville Books.

May, Todd. 2015. *Nonviolent Resistance: A Philosophical Introduction.* Cambridge: Polity.

Nagler, Michael N. *The Search for a Nonviolent Future: A Promise of Peace for Ourselves, Our Families, and Our World.* Maui: Inner Ocean.

Narey, Martin. 2011. *The Narey Report on Adoption.* London: The Times.

National Institute on Drug Abuse. 2014. *Drug Facts: High School and Youth Trends.* Revised January. Accessed May 28, 2015. http://www.drugabuse.gov/publications/drugfacts/high-school-youth-trends.

New York State Office of Children's and Family Services (NYSOCFS). n.d. *Foster Care Rates.* Accessed May 28, 2015. http://ocfs.ny.gov/main/Rates/FosterCare/rates/Default.asp.

———. n.d. *Definitions of Child Abuse and Maltreatment.* Accessed May 28, 2015. http://ocfs.ny.gov/main/cps/critical.asp.

———. 2014. *Child Care Market Rates 2014–2015.* Accessed May 28, 2015. http://ocfs.ny.gov/main/policies/external/OCFS_2014/LCMs/14-OCFS-LCM-03%20Child%20Care%20Market%20Rates%20%202014-2015.pdf.

Ofshe, Richard, and Ethan Watters. 1994. *Making Monsters: False Memories, Psycholtherapy and Sexual Hysteria.* New York: Charles Scribner's Sons.

Pecora, Peter J., Ronald C. Kessler, Jason Williams, Kirk O'Brien, A. Chris Downs, Diana English, James White, Eva Hiripi, Catherine Roller White, Tamera

Wiggins, and Kate Holmes. 2005. *Improving Family Foster Care: Findings from the Northwest Foster Care Alumni Study.* Seattle, WA: Foster Care Alumni Studies.

Pinker, Stephen. 2012. *The Better Angels of Our Nature: Why Violence Has Declined.* London: Penguin.

Pollard, John K. 1987. *Self-Parenting: The Complete Guide to Your Inner Conversations.* Malibu, CA: The Self-Parenting Program.

Rifkin, Jeremy. 2009. *The Empathic Civilization: The Race to Global Consciousness in a World of Crisis.* New York: Jeremy Tarcher/Penguin.

Rosenberg, Marshall B. 2003. *Nonviolent Communication: A Language of Life.* Encinitas, CA: Puddle Dancer.

———. 2005a. *We Can Work it Out: Resolving Conflicts Peacefully and Powerfully.* Encinitas, CA: Puddle Dancer.

———. 2005b. *Raising Children Compassionately: Parenting the Nonviolent Communication Way.* Encinitas, CA: Puddle Dancer.

Ruddick, Sara. 1989, 1995. *Maternal Thinking: Toward a Politics of Peace.* Boston, MA: Beacon Press.

Rutter, Michael. 1981. *Maternal Deprivation Reassessed.* London: Penguin.

Simpkins, C. Alexander, and Annellen M. Simpkins. 2011. *Meditation and Yoga in Psychotherapy: Techniques for Clinical Practice.* Hoboken: John Wiley and Sons.

———. 2012. *Zen Meditation in Psychotherapy; Techniques for Clinical Practice.* Hoboken: John Wiley and Sons.

Statista. 2015. "Children in Foster Placements in England (UK) as of March 31 from 2010 to 2014." Accessed May 28, 2015. http://www.statista.com/statistics/375728/foster-children-england-timeline/.

Straus, Murray A., with Denise A. Donnelly. 1994, 2001. *Beating the Devil Out of Them: Corporal Punishment in American Families and Its Effects on Children.* New Brunswick: Transaction.

United States Department of Agriculture (USDA). 2013. *Parents Projected to Spend $241,080 to Raise a Child in 2012, According to USDA Report.* Release No. 0160.13. Accessed May 28, 2015. http://www.usda.gov/wps/portal/usda/usdahome?contentid=2013/08/0160.xml.

United States Department of Health & Human Services Administration for Children and Families Administration on Children, Youth and Families Children's Bureau (USDHHS). 1997. *Adoption and Safe Families Act. 105-89.* http://www.naswdc.org/archives/advocacy/updates/1997/safeadop.htm.

———. 2014. *The AFCARS Report.* Accessed May 12, 2015. http://www.acf.hhs.gov/sites/default/files/cb/afcarsreport21.pdf.

———. 2015. *Child Maltreatment 2013.* Washington, DC. Accessed April 30, 2015. http://www.acf.hhs.gov/programs/cb/research-data-technology/statistics-research/child-maltreatment.

Vicarious Trauma Institute. 2013. "What is Vicarious Trauma?" Accessed May 28, 2015. http://www.vicarioustrauma.com/whatis.html.

Wesley, Susannah. 1997. *The Complete Writings.* Oxford: Oxford University Press.

Young Minds. *Mental Health Statistics.* Accessed May 28, 2015. http://www.youngminds.org.uk/training_services/policy/mental_health_statistics.

Index

abuse, 7, 16–19, 43, 61, 87, 90, 99, 100, 102, 122, 141–5, 152. *See also* substance abuse
abused teens, 55
acting to heal abuse, 93
a. of carer by cared-for child, 131
child a. linked to drug/alcohol abuse, 26
child a. mirrors abused women, 20
child's faithfulness toward abuser, 129
domestic/spousal, 110
emotional/verbal, 13, 15, 91, 116, 118
and foster care, 5, 6, 22–25, 33, 47
lack of empathy and self-control in a. children, 135
of nonhuman animals, 92
punishment and, 109, 111
sexual, 11, 15, 22, 24, 28, 29, 69, 75
statistics, 2, 3
adopt(ees)(ion), 8, 61, 95
court-ordered contact with birth parents, 102
disrupted, 98–101
factors in successful, 96, 98
foster children freed for, 17
preadoption, 100
training for potential
UK a. laws, 9
US statistics on, 4
when adoption is not an option, 97
Adoption and Safe Families Act, 97, 158
aggression, 59, 61
alcohol abuse/alcoholism, 7, 26, 53, 72, 76–8, 97, 100
anxiety, 30, 55, 122
Aristotle, 85, 86, 125, 132
attachment, 15–7, 48, 54, 61, 63
to adoptive family, 96, 99
cause of suffering, 132

Attachment and Loss Trilogy (Bowlby)
autonomic nervous system (ANS), 147, 148

bathing (showering), 31, 32, 48, 58, 101
beneficence. *See* goodness
birth children of foster parents, 33
body consciousness (somaesthetics), 149
boundaries, 84, 112–116

car(e)(ing), 7, 87, 89, 90, 128, 129
c. for abused children, 6
empathy, self-control, and, 135
for foster children, 8, 22, 33, 99, 123, 125, 133, 162
foster parents' c. for self, 139–53
nonviolent, 23, 157
parental, 2, 7, 48, 49, 61
child maltreatment. *See* abuse
Clinton Act. *See* Adoption and Safe Families Act
clothing allowance, 31, 161
compassion fatigue (Second-Hand Shock Syndrome), 140,141
Confucius, 85
consequences, 124
c. of disrupted empathic growth, 61
c. of harmful actions, 131
imposed by schools, 65
c. of rejection or failure, 126
for rule breaking, 84, 117
Conscientization (consciousness raising), 92
consideration, 127, 135
sexual, 75
courage, 86, 123, 125, 126
criminal justice system, 20, 28, 37, 40, 43, 82, 126, 127

depression, 15, 71, 122, 133, 142
determinist view of human nature, 61
distrust (mistrust), 16, 122
drug abuse. *See* substance abuse

The Empathic Civilization (Rifkin), 59
empathic concern, 60, 61
empathy, 47, 59–62, 92, 153
  "controlled" e., 143
  teaching e., 62, 73, 135
  and self-control/discipline, 115, 116, 120
  and violence, 25, 119
equality, 41–4, 111, 123, 126
ethics, 81–93

fairness, 39, 41, 83, 87, 123, 126, 127
faithfulness, 123, 129
father(ing)(s)
  as distant provider, 48
  God as intolerant father figure, 113
  male ownership of children, 110
  paternal attachment, 16
  violent, 12
  who abandon children, 7
fear(fulness)(s), 16, 25, 64, 122, 155
  of foster children, 30, 50, 51
  of the rod, 57
dignity, 42–4, 111
discipline, 60, 67, 113, 115
  Hobbesean view, 57
  and nonviolence, 112
  parental, 26
  self-discipline, 114
  as synonym for punishment, 58, 87, 88, 107, 110
food, 66–68, 104, 148, 159
  f.-deprivation and security, 51–3, 55, 136
  drip-feed or grazing approach to, 116
  moderation in eating, 132–3
forgiveness (with reparation), 123, 130, 131
foster carer(s)
  abuse allegations against, 5, 23, 24
  aging out, 98
  birth children of, 33
  burnout in, 146
  character traits of, 47, 123, 25, 29, 31

compassion fatigue in, 141
  dealing with tantrums, 118
  dealing with traumatic history of foster children, 33, 91, 152
  empathizing with foster children, 47
  facilitating visits with legal parents
  meditation for, 148, 9
  monetary allowance/reimbursement for, 161–3
  motivation of, 22, 126, 161
  re-parenting role of, 67, 85
  respite care for, 151
  role modeling virtues, 132, 133
  shortage 1, 4, 158, 9
  single parent as, 144
foster children, 6, 10, 22, 163
  fears of, 30
  institutionalization of, 78
  psychiatric diagnoses among, 71
  sexually active, 75
  visits with legal parents, 101, 102

generosity, 35, 127
goodness (beneficence), 57, 123, 124, 132
good will, 38, 124
gratefulness, 33, 123, 131, 132

hatred, 122
Hobbes, Thomas, 40, 56, 57, 61

justice, 41, 123, 126–8
  and school suspensions, 65
juvenile delinquent (JD), 28

Kant, Immanuel, 42, 43, 83, 84, 124
kindness (gentleness), 61, 81, 86, 87, 90, 123, 127, 128, 135, 146

letting go, 130–2
Love as a Guide to Morals (Fitz-Gibbon), 122

MacIntyre, Alasdair, 85
Maslow, Abraham, 47, 50, 51, 62
  M.'s hierarchy, 55, 56
Maternal Deprivation Reassessed (Rutter)
meditation, 146–50, 153
Mill, John Stuart, 124
Miller, Vicki Carpel, 139

mindfulness, 123, 131, 146–50, 153
missing person reports, 69
moderation, 123, 132, 133
mothers, 48
  birth, 21
  foster, 49
  teenage, 7

neglect, 4–8, 14, 15, 17, 22, 23, 24, 28, 29,
  33, 43, 54, 61, 87, 90, 115, 116, 122, 126,
  129, 132, 142, 144, 145, 155
  re-parenting neglected children, 47
  statistics, 2, 3
Neo-Aristotelianism, 85
nonharm (non-maleficence, ahimsa), 41,
  122, 123, 125
non-maleficence. See nonharm
nonviolen(ce)(tism), 6, 11, 23, 41, 44, 45,
  88–90, 92, 93, 101, 107–120
  intentional, 91
  nonviolent habits and virtues, 121–137
  nonviolent reparenting, 47, 61, 87
Nonviolence in Theory and Practice
  (Holmes), 45
nurturance, 49, 62
The Search for a Nonviolent Future
  (Nagler), 44

obsession, 59

pacifism vs. nonviolentism, 45
paranoia, 59
permanence, 95
person in need of supervision (PINS), 28
planned parenthood, 75
Pink Collar Workers (Howe), 48
post traumatic stress disorder (PTSD),
  71, 139, 142
protection, 49, 62
psychiatric diagnoses among foster children, 71
punishment, 83, 84. See also consequences
  corporal (physical), 2, 26, 39, 58, 60,
    108–10, 112, 113, 115
  corporal replaced by more humane, 40,
    43
  effective, 42
  excessive
  foster care rules regarding, 87, 88

and suicide, 111
and violence as, 18, 19, 117

reactive attachment disorder, 71. See also
  attachment
reciprocation, 89
rejection, 54, 126, 155
reparation. See forgiveness
re-parenting, nonviolent, 11, 47–50, 52,
  56, 58, 61, 62, 75, 81, 85, 87, 91–93,
  101, 120–25, 128, 129, 135, 140, 146,
  148, 155, 158
respite care, 151
returning home, 95, 101
Ruddick, Sara, 47, 62, 89
  Maternal Thinking, 48, 49, 128
The Search for a Nonviolent Future
  (Nagler), 44

Second Hand Shock Syndrome. See compassion fatigue; see also post traumatic
  stress disorder
self-control, 49, 61, 62, 114–16, 119, 120,
  135. See also self-discipline
sex in the foster home, 74, 75
  s. abuse, 15, 22, 24, 28, 29, 69, 75. See also
    abuse
self-discipline, 114, 115. See also
  self-control
sharing, 33, 35, 98, 104, 137
siblings
  caring for toddlers as well as newborn,
    61
smoking, 65, 77
  rules for foster teens who smoke, 76
  second-hand smoke, 139
social contract theory, 40
stealing, 9, 72–4, 100, 129
substance (drug) abuse, 7, 15, 63, 72, 76,
  78, 101, 132, 136
suicide, 71, 99, 111
suspensions from school, 65, 66
sympathy, 59, 60, 61. See also empathy

teenage mothers, 7
teleology, elective, 86
training, 49, 62
  foster care training, 47, 87, 141, 152,
    158, 162

trauma, 4, 18, 19, 21, 27, 28, 33, 65, 95, 98, 99. *See also* compassion fatigue; post traumatic stress disorder (PTSD)
psychological effects of direct trauma, 139
traumatic memory, 25
vicarious, 142–4
of violent rejection, 54

values, 42, 59, 61, 81–3, 85–7, 92, 93, 121, 122 , 125
vegetarianism as symbol of nonviolence, 92, 133–7
violence, 12, 13, 52, 125, 126, 151. *See also* nonviolen(ce)(tism); pacifism vs. nonviolentism
against foster children, 2, 6, 11, 27, 47, 50, 61, 87, 92, 93, 101, 129, 152, 155, 156
Christian, 89
v. crime, 79
culture of, 25
effectiveness of, 44
emotional, 14
four loci of, 18
guilt and, 19
morality of, 40, 41, 43

myths of, 41, 42, 152
nonviolent foster care, 93, 115, 116, 159, 160
as punishment, 108–11, 114, 118, 120, 158
sanctioned, 37–9, 83, 90
sexual, 117
shock value of, 91
spousal, 53
structural/systemic, 15, 17, 20, 21, 157
verbal, 13
v. foster children, 66, 67, 100, 122
virtual, 26
Violence and Nonviolence (Gan), 41
virtues, nonviolent, 6, 86, 121, 122–37, 157
v. ethics, 85
twelve v. of love, 122
visit(ation)(s), 21
with birth parents, 101–3
CPS v., 19, 23
maltreatment during, 5
with prospective adoptive parents, 95, 95
supervised/unsupervised, 53, 54
foster children's v. with friends, 69

CPSIA information can be obtained
at www.ICGtesting.com
Printed in the USA
LVOW04s1104140816

500335LV00022B/809/P